FIVE
MINUTE
CHALLENGE
#2

FIVE MINUTE CHALLENGE #2

KEN WEBER

Stoddart

Published in 1998 by Stoddart Publishing Co. Limited
34 Lesmill Road, Toronto, Canada M3B 2T6

Distributed in Canada by General Distribution Services Limited
325 Humber College Blvd., Toronto, Canada M9W 7C3
Tel. (416) 213-1919 Fax (416) 213-1917
E-mail customer.service@ccmailgw.genpub.com

Distributed in the U.S. by General Distribution Services Inc.
85 River Rock Drive, Suite 202, Buffalo, New York 14207
Toll-free tel. 1-800-805-1083 Toll-free fax 1-800-481-6207
E-mail gdsinc@genpub.com

02 01 00 99 98 1 2 3 4 5

Cataloguing in Publication Data

Weber, K. J. (Kenneth Jerome), 1940–
Five-minute challenge #2

ISBN 0-7737-5989-1

1. Questions and answers. I. Title.

GV1507.Q5W42 1998   031.02   C98-931483-9

Brief portions of the text appeared in different form in
the author's 1995 book *Did the Corinthians Ever Write Back?*

Cover design: Bill Douglas @ The Bang
Text design: Tannice Goddard
Computer graphics: Mary Bowness

Printed and bound in Canada

*We gratefully acknowledge the Canada Council for the Arts and the
Ontario Arts Council for their support of our publishing program.*

To the AWFFLS
May they reign!

◁ Introduction ▷

A typical trivia buff is marked by three delightful qualities. The first, naturally, is curiosity. But not ordinary, run-of-the-mill curiosity. A trivia buff's curiosity is passionate, consuming, and never satisfied. Take the Wright brothers, for example – Orville and Wilbur. Everybody knows they powered an airplane into the sky at Kitty Hawk in 1903. What the trivia buff wants to know is, *which brother flew the plane?* Or the world's first phone call, when Alexander Graham Bell's assistant suddenly heard his boss's voice come through the equipment they were working on. The words, very famous now, were "Mr. Watson, come here. I want you." Interesting, sure, but a buff's curiosity cries out: *why did Bell want him?*

Movies, as you might expect, are an Eden of curious delights. Sports, too. Indeed, the two often work together. Boxing, for example, has been featured more than any other sport in the history of movie-making. Tell that to trivia buffs and they'll immediately say something like *"Fantastic! What's number two?"* Answer that one and you'll see another of the three defining qualities: an infinite capacity for wonder and fascination. True buffs will be genuinely pleased to learn that horse racing is number two, and utterly intrigued by the fact that baseball is way down in fifth place, and that golf comes in behind wrestling!

By this point you'll see a smile, for the third special quality is a trivia buff's great sense of humor. Curiosity, wonder, and laughter. Great qualities to have, and that's why I'm willing to go out on a limb and claim that reading *Five-Minute Challenge #2* could be really good for you. For sure it will make you chuckle. (An exclusive news report on the Wrights' big day was rejected by *Scientific American*, so the author sold it to a beekeepers' magazine.) And it will definitely fascinate. (Despite the conventional wisdom, Bell's call wasn't the first. A German inventor named Reis had a working model of the telephone fifteen years earlier.) As for curiosity, *Five-Minute Challenge #2* offers treats like these: what's the name of the legendary Swiss hero who shot an apple off his son's head? Sure, William Tell. *What was his son's name?* Where does John Brown's body "lie a-moldering"? Right, in the grave. *Where's the grave?* A dog of mixed breed is called what? Yes, a mongrel. *What's a cat of mixed breed called?*

If you open this book at any page, you'll see that each offering follows this double-question principle. First there's an ordinary trivia question (e.g.: *An animal with two feet is a biped. What's an animal with four feet?*). That's followed by the answer (*A quadruped*) and then a challenge (*What's a pinniped?*). Turn the page and you get the answer to the challenge (*An animal with flippers*), followed by a short journey into trivia guaranteed to appeal to a buff's sense of wonder and sense of humor. The journey following the pinniped question, for example, offers gems like this one. After the filming of *The Canine Detective* (1936), in which Rin Tin Tin Jr. catches an entire band of crooks single-handed (well, single-*pawed*), the star was returned to his master's home in Malibu Beach. Here he managed to sleep blissfully the next day while a break-and-enter team took the whole afternoon to clean the place out!

There are one hundred of these appeals to curiosity, wonder, and humor in *Five-Minute Challenge #2*. Try a few. You may discover you've been a genuine trivia buff all along and didn't realize it!

Q: His boss is M. His CIA friend is Felix Leiter. And he has the best-known code number in the movies. What is it?

A: Yes, 007 ("Double-O-Seven").

The Challenge

Q: What is the significance of that number to James Bond?

A: **The double zero authorizes him to kill.** Ironically, the one movie in which M takes away this authority is called *Licence to Kill* (1989). United Artists had planned to call it *Licence Revoked*, but a market-research survey told them that less than 20 percent of the American public know what "revoked" means!

Titles are often a delicate matter, especially when movies are released in several countries at once. Sometimes the issue is pretty straightforward. For example, a 1960 British movie, *Never Take Sweets from a Stranger*, came out in North America as *Never Take Candy from a Stranger*. But that's English to English. When there's a shift in language as well as geography, the risk level elevates. *City Slickers* (1991) was a hit everywhere but France, where distributors ran *Life, Love, and Cows* across their marquees. Since "grease" translates into Spanish as *"grasa,"* a word many Spanish speakers use for "fat," the 1978 movie *Grease* became *Vaselina* in Venezuela.

Releasing Hollywood movies in Hong Kong can be a major challenge. *Not as a Stranger* (1955) appeared there as *The Heart of a Lady as Pure as a Full Moon over the Place of Medical Salvation*. Not much different in Indonesia, where, in the same year, *I'll Cry Tomorrow* was offered as *To Relieve Yourself from the Grief of Your Passions*. But it may be decades before the industry matches the release of the 1992 Hollywood feature *White Men Can't Jump* in Italy. It became a hit there, as *White Men Don't Know How to Stick It In*. Quite possibly basketball is not as popular in Italy as other sports.

2

Q: In the year 490 B.C., a messenger named Pheidippides (a.k.a. Phidippides) made a long-distance run to Athens — barefoot — to bring news that the Persians had been defeated in a mighty battle. His great run is commemorated today in a type of footrace that we call what?

A: Right, a marathon, after Marathon, the site of the battle, and the point where Pheidippides took off.

The Challenge

Q: How long is the Olympic marathon?

A: **26 miles, 385 yards,** or 42,195 meters. It started out in 1896 at 40,000 m, but was changed in 1908, in London, so competitors could lap the stadium and finish in front of the Royal Box. The distance has remained that way since.

The change in 1908 caused far less flap that year than the race itself. Crowd favorite Dorando Pietri of Italy was leading at the finish, but once in the stadium he ran the wrong way. Officials turned him around and he collapsed. They revived him and he collapsed again. After the fifth drop, they *carried* him across the finish line — just ahead of American John Hayes. Although the gold did go to Hayes, the crowd was not satisfied until Queen Alexandra presented Pietri with a special gold cup the next day.

This was tame compared to the 1904 marathon in St. Louis, where first place went to Fred Lorz (U.S.A.) until it was discovered he'd done over half the race in a car! Fourth place went to Félix Carvajal (Cuba), who, on the way to St. Louis, had lost all his money in a crap game in New Orleans, and arrived at the start line in civvies and street shoes. Carvajal might even have won had he not diverted into an orchard for some green apples which gave him cramps. In ninth place was the first-ever black African Olympian, Lentauw (no other name given). He looked like the winner until two large dogs chased him off on a long detour. Even the official winner, Thomas Hicks (U.S.A.), would have been an IOC nightmare in today's show. Along the route his handlers topped him up regularly with a mix of egg white, brandy, and strychnine.

3

Q: In 1884, the International Prime Meridian Conference (held in Washington, DC, but very much the inspiration of a Canadian, Sir Sandford Fleming) divided the world into time zones, which we continue to use today. How many zones are there?

A: Right, twenty-four.

The Challenge

Q: Are all twenty-four time zones identical in size?

A: Yes. Each zone is 15° of longitude wide, but many countries choose to make modifications. For example, Iran, Afghanistan, Myanmar, and Sri Lanka all have half-hour zones. Nepal is forty minutes off the mark. India, which actually covers two time zones, decided to have only one. It split the one-hour difference and put the whole country into a half-hour zone. In Saudi Arabia, at sunset, the clocks are reset to midnight. Then there's Russia, which first tried Daylight Saving Time in 1930 and then decided it would be less confusing if things just stayed that way. Canada, which has six time zones to begin with, has one province (Newfoundland) in a half-hour zone and another (Saskatchewan) which opts out when the rest of the country goes to Daylight Saving. Not hard to see why heads of state prefer to fly in their own aircraft!

In 1884, despite vehement objections from France, the Prime Meridian Conference voted to use Greenwich, England, which is at 0° longitude, as the base point for Greenwich Mean Time (GMT). It further agreed that zones to the east are ahead of GMT, and those to the west are behind. The island of Malta is in the GMT+1 zone, but should you adjust your watch before landing there, you may wish to reflect on the fact that many churches in Malta have two clocks, one set correctly, the other deliberately set wrong in order to confuse the devil. Whether the practice actually works is uncertain. In 1958, *Life* magazine published a nine-page "interview" with the devil and he didn't mention it. But then, the interview didn't ask his views on time zones either.

Q: "M" words #1: what "m" word describes a dog of mixed and uncertain breed?

A: Yes, mongrel.

The Challenge

Q: "M" words #2: what "m" word describes a cat of mixed and uncertain breed?

A: **Moggy,** a term from Australia, where a song entitled "He's Nobody's Moggy Now" expresses satisfaction at seeing a dead one on the road (suggesting that moggies may not be all that popular there).

On the plus side, moggies and their kin are natural enemies of rats, a species that could do with a few more enemies to keep things in balance. Rats can scale brick walls, tread water for up to three days, eat through lead pipe and cinder blocks, survive a fall from five stories. Experiments carried out while animal rights activists were looking the other way, have demonstrated that after a toss from five stories up, rats scurry away unharmed about 80 percent of the time.

Rats can survive without water longer than camels can (which may explain why there are more rats than camels in central Nevada). And unlike mongrels and moggies, rats seem capable of music appreciation. In 1970, at University College in Cardiff, Wales, researchers found that rats preferred to hang out by the Mozart tapedeck rather than the Schoenberg one – although even for a rat, that would hardly be a difficult choice.

Whether rats have an equal sensitivity for poetry has yet to be discovered. It is known, however, that during the years 1843 to 1850, Queen Victoria paid her poet laureate, William Wordsworth, less than she paid the royal rat catcher. If nothing else, this proves there is justice in the world, for a quick skim of Wordsworth's output for this period reveals that he definitely did not earn his creative keep. (It's not known whether he caught any rats, but he did have a moggy.)

Q: What girl at the *Daily Planet* was reporter Clark Kent fond of but too shy to approach?

A: Sure, Lois Lane.

The Challenge

Q: What girl on a Brazilian beach was composer Antonio Carlos Jobim fond of but too shy to approach?

A: **The girl from Ipanema.** Jobim, Brazil's best-loved composer, used to watch Helo Pinheiro walk on the beach but was too shy to talk to her. It was 1963. He was 27; she was 17. They never spoke until his song *The Girl from Ipanema* became a worldwide hit.

The song has been recorded almost 200 times, and in several languages. As things stand right now, none of these are Middle English, the language of Chaucer – which may be just as well, for in Chaucer's time, "girl" was used to describe a young person of either sex. On the other hand, "girl" doesn't appear at all in the King James Version of the Bible. For that matter, nor does the word "cat." "Dog," however, appears eighteen times.

Such matters of etymology clearly did not bother Paramount Studios, for the moguls there went to great lengths to make silent screen actress Clara Bow into the "It Girl" after her successful movie *It* in 1927. Hollywood also took a shot at making Gary Cooper the "It Boy," but it didn't stick. Cooper objected in any case, arguing that his popularity needed no such help. Whether or not that's so is debatable: he led the Quigley Poll as top male box office draw only once in his career – a tie with Abbott and Costello! Clara Bow was top female draw twice. That's Dolly Parton's number, too. And Elizabeth Taylor's. Doris Day, however, has been top draw *seven* times.

During composer Jobim's funeral procession in 1994, in Rio de Janeiro, a tall and tanned middle-aged lady suddenly broke from the crowd, silently tossed a red rose onto the coffin, and strode away. The girl from Ipanema was saying goodbye.

Q: In April 1961, what Caribbean island was invaded from the U.S. (but not by U.S. troops)?

A: Yes, Cuba, in the hugely embarrassing Bay of Pigs invasion.

The Challenge

Q: In October 1983, what Caribbean island was invaded from the U.S. (by U.S. troops)?

A: Grenada. A somewhat more successful venture this time for the invaders, although a bit one-sided (total military personnel at the time: U.S., 1,715,132; Grenada, 112). Still, it took a couple of days, partly because the Grenadians had home field advantage and partly because of the U.S. military's application of Murphy's Law. For example, a marine lieutenant on the outskirts of St. George's, the Grenadian capital, after failing repeatedly to get through to a unit on the other side of the city, finally used a pay phone to call his family in the U.S. The family called their local police, who called the Pentagon, who relayed the message to the other unit.

Fortunately, nuclear weapons were not required in this operation, but then, these devices have a Murphy history all their own. Among the scariest examples is the discovery by both Soviet and U.S. technicians after the Cuban missile crisis of October 1962 that their respective ICBMs had electronic faults which could have caused them to launch themselves.

Murphy must have been listening to air force chief Curtis LeMay during the aforementioned crisis. On October 23, LeMay commented, "If there is to be war, there's no better time than the present. We are prepared and 'The Bear' is not." Two days later, a bear climbed the perimeter fence at the U.S. base in Duluth, Minnesota, triggering a sabotage alarm across the Northwest. Somehow, this turned into a nuclear attack alert at Volk Field, Wisconsin, causing B-29 pilots to scramble on a real-thing, no-recall response. Happily, the base commander at Volk telephoned Duluth to get the story straight and was in time to send his staff out onto the runway in their personal cars to prevent a takeoff. After this, Murphy rested.

Q: Alfred Bernhard Nobel (1833–96) is known for the prizes that have been awarded in his name every year since 1901. To establish the awards, Nobel bequeathed a fortune of about $9 million. Part of his money had been earned through shrewd investments like the Baku oil fields of Russia, but most of it came from an invention that shook the world – literally. What was this invention?

A: Sure, dynamite. He also invented ballistite (a smokeless gunpowder) and a form of synthetic rubber, but dynamite was the big one.

The Challenge

Q: Invention was not exactly new to the Nobel family. About the time Alfred was born, his father, Immanuel, had developed a blowup item of his own that made him rich also. What did Immanuel Nobel invent?

A. **Floating sea mines.** Prior to the invention of dynamite, nitroglycerine was the explosive of choice, but it was so dangerously unstable that many countries had banned it. After long and complicated experimentation, Alfred found that combining nitro with ordinary clay did the job, and soon factories were churning out "Nobel's safety powder." Ironically, Nobel always conceived of dynamite solely as a benefit to humankind. Even after Prussian engineers used it in bombs, he naively clung to the belief that if every nation's military did so, war would be simply too horrible to contemplate. It took a monumental goof by a Swedish newspaper to shake him up. When Alfred turned to the obituary column one morning in 1888 to read about his brother, Ludwig, he was shocked not only to find his own obit instead, but even more to find himself described as the late "merchant of death." In order to erase that notion from his legacy, he began the process that created the Nobel prizes.

Whether or not such a move was needed is unclear, for human memory seems to be very selective in matters of invention. For sure, we all recall Bell, and Edison (who did not *invent* the lightbulb), and even the earl of Condom, personal physician to Charles II. But who among us remembers Peter Durand, of the sealable tin can (1810), or Joseph Block (the whistling tea kettle, 1921), or Arthur Wynne (the crossword puzzle, 1913)? In all likelihood, there are many inventors in the world like Italian chemist Ascanio Sobrero. In 1847, he produced the world's first drop of nitroglycerine. When it exploded with shattering violence, he realized its potential in warfare and abruptly stopped his research. Others, as we now know, carried on.

Q: The first uniform number ever to be retired by the New York Yankees (Number 4) was worn by a first baseman known as the "Iron Man." Who was the Iron Man?

A: Yes, Lou (Henry Louis) Gehrig. He was dubbed "Iron Man" for playing in 2,130 consecutive games, all the while developing a reputation as one of baseball's best players.

The Challenge

Q: In the same league, the Detroit Tigers had a player who is often described as not just one of the best players in the sport, but possibly *the* best: Ty Cobb. Yet the Tigers never retired Cobb's number. Why not?

A: **He didn't have one.** Ty (Tyrus Raymond) Cobb's playing career with the Tigers predated the practice of putting numbers on uniforms.

Cobb and the Tigers enjoy other distinctions in baseball history, such as responsibility for possibly the weirdest pro baseball game ever. Early in the 1912 season, Cobb jumped into the stands to beat up a fan who had been heckling him. Not unusual behavior for Cobb, who was known to beat up delivery boys, elevator operators, and even his roommates, but in this case it was a bit extreme, since the fan in question had no arms. Cobb was turfed from the game and suspended, and in a rather rare display of support, his fellow Tigers — who, understandably, were not overfond of him — went on strike. Without missing a beat, the Tigers' owner fielded nine volunteers off the street for the next game (with Philadelphia). The volunteers lost 24–2, but that's not all. One of the temporary Tigers had an exceptionally long name, which the scorekeeper either could not spell or could not fit on the scorecard, so the name went into the lineup as "L'n'h's'r." To this day, in a sport obsessed with record-keeping, no one has any idea who L'n'h's'r was. He is known in baseball lore simply as "Four Apostrophes."

Only marginally less weird is the "four teeth" pregame display in 1939 by Cleveland Indians catcher Joe Sprinz. As part of a publicity stunt, he agreed to catch a ball dropped from an airplane at 1,000 feet (305 m). Whether he was unaware of Sir Isaac Newton's work from centuries before or chose to ignore it, Sprinz made the catch holding his mitt just above his face. (Not hard to figure out the rest, is it?)

Q: When Wild Bill Hickok was shot in the back of the head by Jack McCall during a game of five card draw, he was holding a pair of aces and a pair of eights. What has this famous poker hand come to be called?

A: Right: "Dead Man's Hand." The game was in Deadwood Gulch, South Dakota – which seems rather appropriate – and Hickok was holding the two black eights and the two black aces.

The Challenge

Q: It was *five* card draw. What was Hickok's fifth card?

A. **The jack of diamonds.** Hickok is famed as town marshal of Abilene, Kansas, although he was fired after only a year. His salary was $150 a month plus 50 cents for each unlicensed dog he shot. Although there is no record of the number of dogs put away, he did manage to shoot his own deputy by accident. Hickok's fame as a gunslinger stands on equally shaky ground. In his first authenticated fight, he shot an unarmed man from behind a curtain.

James Butler Hickok sported a flowing mustache, possibly to divert attention from his long nose and protruding upper lip – or possibly from his nickname, "Duck Bill." It must have worked, for journalist Henry M. Stanley was inspired to describe him as "[as] handsome a specimen of a man as could be found," but then, Stanley, not unlike many journalists, seems to have had his very own view of reality. In 1871, he set out on his famous expedition to find the missing African explorer David Livingstone – except that Livingstone wasn't lost! When Stanley found him, in November that year, Livingstone knew just where he was: at Ujiji (which, if you want to find the spot for yourself, is right across Lake Tanganyika from Fizi and a bit north of Sumbawahga).

Stanley made himself famous with the discovery, though, and then seemed to develop a passion for finding others who weren't lost either. In 1885, he "found" Emin Pasha, the governor of the Sudan, relaxing in the Ruwenzori Mountains of the Congo. However, the Pasha, a German named Eduard Schnitzer, was having a perfectly agreeable time and had no wish whatsoever to leave. So the two drank champagne on the shores of Lake Albert-Nyasa and Stanley went home alone. His journals don't tell us if they played poker.

Q: What's longer, an eon or an era?

A: Yes, an eon.

The Challenge

Q: What's longer, a period or an epoch?

A: **A period.** Unless you have tried to get your shirts laundered in Ireland, these distinctions have likely never played a major role in your life. Still, in the interests of ready reference, here are some data to engrave on the back of your Rolex.

There are three eons in the geologic time scale: the Archean, the Proterozoic, and the Phanerozoic (the last, about 248 million years long, being favored by Irish drycleaners). There are four eras, the most familiar one to non-geologists being the Precambrian, and fifteen periods. The best-known period, thanks to Steven Spielberg, is the Jurassic. However, the one we're in right now is the Quaternary. As for our current epoch, it's the Holocene, which began about ten thousand years ago. Strangely, our own epoch is less familiar to us than the one immediately prior to it, the Pleistocene. That was when glaciers made it impossible to get your shirts done no matter where you went. As for how many epochs there are, geologists are not in complete agreement, because some make distinctions like *early*, *middle*, and *late* while others don't. For your Rolex engraving, however, plan on over thirty.

Before Charles Darwin and others dragged Western culture kicking and screaming into new ways of thinking in the late nineteenth century, just about everyone agreed with the calculations of James Ussher (1581–1656), Anglican bishop of Meath, who pinpointed Earth's creation to October 23, 4004 B.C. The only modification to his formula came from the vice-chancellor of Cambridge, John Lightfoot (1602–75), who, not to be outdone in matters of scientific insight, narrowed the timing of the Creation down to October 23, 4004 B.C., *at 9 a.m.*

Q: The jail in Reading, England, has at least two claims to fame. One is that when it first opened, guards discovered that the locks in the holding room for new prisoners had been installed on the inside! The other claim, of course, is housing a well-known poet and *bon vivant* for a stretch of hard labor from 1895 to 1897. He later wrote "The Ballad of Reading Gaol" (anonymously, and not necessarily as a tribute). The poet?

A: Sure, Oscar Wilde. He had an affair with Alfred Douglas, a young English lord, and was convicted of sodomy.

The Challenge

Q: What is Wilde's real name?

A: **Oscar Fingal O'Flahertie Wills.** While he was not really "the original Bohemian" as he is sometimes called, Wilde's eccentricities made him an especially noticeable alternative lifestyle figure. A leader of the "art for art's sake" movement, he became famous for his wit and flamboyant behavior (not to mention his ego, as demonstrated on a trip to the U.S. where he told a customs officer he had nothing to declare but his genius!).

In a sense, Wilde was the author of his own misfortune, for in choosing young Alfred, he got a partner whose father not only was a powerful Scottish peer but had fame in his own right. Sir John Sholto Douglas was the eighth marquis of Queensberry, credited with revolutionizing the popular sport of boxing with new rules like requiring gloves, pausing the fight every three minutes, and declaring eye-gouging illegal — which had the effect of making ringside seats a more sanitary and agreeable venue. Wilde chose to tangle with Sir John and sued for libel, but the suit fizzled when his lifestyle was made public, and that's when he went to Reading jail (in his case, *gaol*). Ostracized in England, after doing his time Wilde adopted the name Sebastian Melmoth and moved to Paris, where his life ended in a cheap hotel (on the Left Bank, where else?).

He died while sipping champagne he couldn't afford, but even *in extremis* was capable of memorable wit. His final quip:* "I am dying beyond my means."

(*As a last word, Wilde is also credited with "Either this wallpaper goes or I do.")

Q: Can a human survive being struck by lightning?

A: Yes. One of the more dramatic proofs is the case of R. C. Sullivan of the Virginia Forest Service. Between 1942 and 1977, he was hit seven times and walked — well, on a couple of occasions he was carried — away!

The Challenge

Q: Statistically, where is the best place for a human to survive a hit from a bolt of lightning?

A: Anywhere but at home, it seems. Just over 50 percent of lightning-caused deaths occur indoors. Mr. Sullivan, however, took all but one of his hits in the great outdoors, so who knows!

That lightning can strike twice, or even more often than that, is not surprising given that during the time it takes you to read this page, about six *thousand* lightning bolts will strike the surface of the planet. If you are an exceptionally slow reader, therefore, you should pay careful attention to the Stanford Research Institute, which estimates that the odds are a million to one against lightning striking a picnic held in a one-quarter-acre (.1-hectare) area of North Dakota between 3 and 4 p.m. on the fourth of July.

Still, even for people who can get to an Independence Day picnic in North Dakota, it's unsettling to realize that what we know about protection against lightning is inexact at best. There's no certainty, for example, that lightning rods really work. (But just in case, NASA has one at the top of the gantry that holds launch vehicles in place.) Good advice, though, is to stay away from trees during a storm; about a third of the victims who become statistics seek shelter that way. Even more persuasive is this datum: in 1989, two rhinos, mating under a tree, were struck in Kruger National Park, South Africa. When they came to, they had lost all interest in their previous activity and slowly wandered off in different directions.

Q: Chinese is the most common first language in the world. What language is number two?

A: Sure, English. And Spanish is third.

The Challenge

Q: What country in the world has the greatest number of first languages?

A. **Papua New Guinea.** By the end of the twentieth century, linguists identified 869 separate *languages* – not dialects – in that country. In the matter of dialects, India gets top billing. Although Hindi is its official language and is number four on the world's most-spoken list, India nevertheless echoes with 845 linguistically distinct ways of getting a point across. Arabic is fifth on the world list of most-spoken languages. Russian, Bengali, Japanese, German, and Portuguese complete the top ten. French doesn't make it. Nor does Italian, which is actually out-spoken by two unofficial Indian languages, Punjabi and Bihari.

With so many languages to choose from, it's curious that the devil limits himself to Greek, Latin, and Hebrew, along with oddly accented English. This information is provided by no less an authority than Cotton Mather, the fire-and-brimstone instigator of the Salem witch trials in 1692. Mather does not tell us whether the devil uses a dictionary, although conceivably, if he did, it would be an English one, for this language has more such aids than any other. The grand lady of the species is the *Oxford English Dictionary*, in which the longest word is pneumonoultramicroscopicsilicovolcanoconiosis, a lung disease, and the longest entry is for the verb set. This latter word – but not the one for a lung disease – can be found in Khalka, the official language of Mongolia, where a dictionary, if you can find one for sale, costs about forty Tugrik.

There is no evidence that the devil has ever appeared for a speaking engagement in Mongolia or Papua New Guinea, although both countries have one of the world's lowest ratios of lawyers to population. These two facts may not necessarily be connected.

Q: "Three on a lucifer" is a bad-luck superstition which has its roots in the Crimean War but did not become widespread until World War I. What's a "lucifer"?

A: Right, a wooden match. The nickname goes back to the first days of match use in the 1820s and '30s, when production versions threw off sparks, burst into flame spontaneously, and — truly satanic — gave off an extremely vile odor.

The Challenge

Q: Why is "three on a lucifer" considered bad luck?

A. **Lighting three cigarettes on a match gave snipers time to take aim.** The superstition, and the phrase, began in the Crimean War when British and French soldiers first picked up cigarette smoking from their Turkish allies and from Russian POWs. By World War I, wooden matches – still called "lucifers" – still smelled pretty bad but were less spontaneous because most were being made with some of the necessary chemistry separated from the match head and instead put on the striking surface. Although paper matches or "matchbooks" were available (since 1892), the trenches of France and Belgium were so wet and soggy that soldiers usually preferred the messy and smelly, but reliable, lucifers. (This was far less the case in the German trenches, where conditions were vastly superior, with raised walkways and even some wallpapered sleeping quarters.)

By World War II, matches had fallen in popularity in favor of lighters, although in the Romanian army there was never a sufficient supply of either. Yet that shortage must have been the least of a Romanian soldier's worries, for according to the *World Book of Odds*, his chances were one in two of being carried off the field. (Compare this to Japan's forces in World War II, which, notwithstanding banzai attacks, had casualty odds of one in seven.)

The matchbook was invented by Joshua Pusey, a U.S. attorney who, possibly just to prove there are limits to inspiration, put the striking surface *inside* the cover! Three years later the Diamond Match Company made the switch that has been with us ever since, and just one year after that, the first advertising – for beer – appeared on the back cover. (Survivors of the Romanian forces reported a beer shortage, too!)

Q: The logo of the modern Olympics is a series of rings in an interlocking pattern. How many rings are there?

A: Right, five.

The Challenge

Q: Each ring is a different color. What are the colors?

A. **Blue, black, yellow, green, and red.** Chosen because at least one of these colors appears in every national flag in the world. Well, almost; check the flags of Qatar and Latvia. Both have an off-purple/brown. Still, these logo colors have lasted longer than some Olympic events. In 1904, for example, medals were awarded for croquet, club swinging, throwing the javelin with two hands, and "plunging" – floating the longest distance in sixty seconds from a standing dive.

Spectators at the 1904 plunging competition must have been at least as thrilled as Canada's ambassador to Argentina was in 1976, when the organizing committee for the Summer Games in Montreal called itself COJO for short. "*Cojo*" is Argentinian slang for sexual activity. Canada struck gold, so to speak, once again at the 1998 Winter Games in Japan, where its athletes wore highly popular hats and jackets prominently displaying the manufacturer's name, Roots, slang for sex in Australia.

Still, when it comes to Olympian embarrassment, the gold medal probably goes to the 1960 pentathlon team from Tunisia. At the Summer Games in Rome, every member of the team fell off their horses in the riding competition, thereby becoming the first-ever Olympic contestants to score zero in an event. In swimming, they came last (one member almost drowned). They were disqualified in fencing because only one could fence and he was illegally used three times. During the pistol shooting they were ordered off the range for endangering the lives of the judges. Only in cross-country running did the team keep from screwing up. When the points were totaled, the Tunisians came seventeenth out of seventeen, scoring half the points of the German team, which came sixteenth.

Tunisia's flag is red and white.

Q: Longitude is one of the two most commonly used dimensions in mapping. What is the other one?

A: Yes, latitude.

The Challenge

Q: When the two are used together, which one comes first?

A° **Latitude.** For example, Fingal's Cave, in the Hebrides, is at roughly 58° N (north *latitude*) and 7° W (west *longitude*). Although composer Felix Mendelssohn knew this when he went there for inspiration in 1830, he wisely used a guide, but then, so did Fingal himself the first time.

Fingal, or Finn MacCool, or Fionn MacCumhail (he was famous as a warrior, not for spelling), was the legendary leader of the Irish Fenians in the third century. Unless you're steeped in the wonder of Irish legend, mention of Fenians is more likely to evoke accounts of the Irish brotherhood that formed in New York in 1857 and reached back into history for its name. Among their other failed endeavors, these Fenians led an invasion force across the Canadian border (at roughly 49° N, 79° W) and after a farcical encounter with the local militia, got drunk and went home. (Other accounts reverse the final sequence, i.e., "went home and got drunk," but these often depend on whether the writer was pro- or anti-Irish.)

Three years later, at 36° N, 6° W, citizens of Algeciras, Spain, heaved a sigh of relief when the Suez Canal opened and they were not crushed by a tidal wave. Doomsayers had warned that because the Red Sea is lower than the Mediterranean, a rush out of the latter into the former would draw a compensating swell from the Atlantic, wiping out the city. As it turned out, Algeciras stayed dry. Not so in one of the host hotels during the opening ceremonies in Cairo (30° N, 6° W), where a too-convivial diplomat fell into a urinal trough and blocked the drain. He was French, and therefore unlikely to have been a Fenian.

Q: Since 1876, consumers have been able to buy this man's ketchup, along with his company's more than fifty-seven varieties of food. The man and the ketchup?

A: Of course, Heinz. H. J. Heinz.

The Challenge

Q: What do the initials H. J. stand for?

A. **Henry John.** Originally, the company he formed with his cousin and brother was called F. & J. Heinz. It became H. J. Heinz in 1888. The famous "57 Varieties" slogan appeared in the mid-1890s and at the time, the company was actually producing sixty-five different products, but H. J. liked the ring of "57" and, well, it was *his* company.

H. J. died in 1919, too soon to hear of a discovery by University of Toronto physics students in the late 1950s. They determined that at room temperature, high-quality ketchup poured at an angle of 45° would take just under eighty years to flow the length of the border between the U.S. and Canada. (Another of H. J.'s misses was the news that the wire of an original Slinky toy is eighty feet (24.4 m) long. Slinkys appeared in 1945.)

Some other essential measurements you can confirm at home:

- From a 3.5-fl.-oz. (100-ml) tube of toothpaste, you can squeeze out 78.7 inches (2 m) of paste – plus or minus 1.2 percent.
- It takes six hours (+/– seven minutes) to play .62 miles (1 km) of audiocassette tape. (Prerequisites are a high-quality sixty-minute tape and a tapedeck that reverses automatically.)
- A standard HB lead pencil can produce a continuous line up to 35.6 miles (55 km) long.

One piece of data you may find very time-consuming to confirm at home, but which has been established by the Gillette Razor company, is that over his three score and ten, the typical male will shave off just under 26.2 feet (8 m) of facial hair.

Q: What bank was established in London's Threadneedle Street in 1694?

A: Yes, the Bank of England.

The Challenge

Q: What bank was established at Moscow's Sklifosovsky Institute in 1931?

A: **A blood bank,** the world's first, although the term "blood bank" was not coined until America's first was set up in Chicago, in 1937. Interestingly, this latter event occurred precisely 270 years after the world's first blood *transfusion*. A British divinity student, Arthur Coga, took in a pint from a sheep in 1667, and became such a social hit that he did it again several times in public demonstrations. Unfortunately, as time went on, Coga developed a reputation for consuming pints of a different nature. This habit, along with his passion for gambling, was blamed on the transfusions, thus removing much of the impetus for further scientific investigation.

Moscow's blood bank was the work of Doctor Sergei Yudin. His efforts were duplicated and much improved upon at New York City's first blood bank, set up in 1940 by Doctor Richard Drew. A major difference between these two founders is that Yudin was a regular and enthusiastic donor, whereas in New York, Drew was not allowed to donate because he was black. It is interesting to speculate whether Yudin's blood would have been acceptable there either, for he was a communist.

Bureaucrats responsible for the rank discrimination in Doctor Drew's case in 1940 clearly chose to ignore a significant racial comparison that the field of biochemistry had made known by that time. Researchers were able to report with confidence that the earwax of the black and the white races have identical characteristics (wet and sticky). The cerumen of the Oriental race, however, tends to be dry and crumbly. As it turns out, the New York agency did not develop a policy on Oriental peoples until 1941.

Q: The date: August 5, 1864. The location: Mobile Bay, Alabama. The commander: David Glasgow Farragut. The phrase: "Damn the torpedoes! . . ." What's the rest of the phrase?

A: Sure, "Full speed ahead!"

The Challenge

Q: Torpedoes as we understand them today were not invented until after the Civil War. So what was Farragut damning?

A. **Beer kegs filled with gunpowder** – what we know as mines.

An Englishman invented the motorized torpedo in 1870, although in 1868, Austria had a working prototype propelled by compressed air. In 1878, the first ship (Turkish) to be sunk by a motorized torpedo (Russian) went to the bottom of the Black Sea. The first torpedo-equipped sub (Greek) sailed in 1886. She was built in Sweden. The first warship (Chilean) to be sunk by a torpedo went down in 1891.

For years, the torpedo was a notoriously unreliable weapon – all for the best, perhaps. Take, for example, the sinking of the mighty German battleship *Bismarck*. Ten British torpedo planes were sent to get her on May 26, 1941, but every one of their "fish" either exploded on hitting the water or made dead aim for the bottom. Just as well, for they were bombing HMS *Sheffield*! This was not unlike a situation off the Scottish coast two days into the war, when a British Avro Anson dove in to drop a pair of 100-pound bombs on a submarine. The bombs bounced off the water and came back up to explode on either side of the Anson, bringing it down in nearby St. Andrew's Bay. The sub was British, so its crew was sufficiently miffed to decline participation in the rescue.

One of the most curious entries in the torpedo file goes to Minoru "Madman" Genda, called "Madman" not for his antics as leader of the Japanese navy's aerobatic team (although the term would have been appropriate, apparently), but because he kept insisting that airplanes with torpedoes could be used to sink battleships. It was Genda who became the principal planner for the attack on Pearl Harbor. The curiosity? In 1962, President Kennedy awarded Genda the U.S. Legion of Merit.

Q: On December 17, 1903, two brothers who normally spent their days making bicycles in Dayton, Ohio, instead made aviation history above a stretch of sand near Kitty Hawk, North Carolina. Who were these brothers?

A: Sure, the Wright brothers, Orville and Wilbur, who are credited with the first sustained flight in a motor-powered air-craft.

The Challenge

Q: Which brother flew the plane?

A: **Orville.** And for the next forty years he flew without a pilot's license!

Orville's famous first was estimated at 120 feet (36.6 meters) from liftoff to touchdown. That's quite a bit less than the wingspan of a Boeing 747, and *estimated* because the Wrights didn't bother to get out the measuring tape until later in the day. Such a statistical omission would never occur today because of a range of items such as the flight recorder, or "black box" (which, as everyone knows, is orange). Mandatory recording technology today not only lays out aeronautical chapter and verse for postflight analysis, it has even enabled researchers to discover that 80.2 percent of pilots involved in an accident were whistling at some point in the last half hour of flight.

The Wrights' fourth and final flight that day, this time with Wilbur at the controls, was measured carefully. In fifty-nine seconds, *Flyer* covered 852 feet (260 m). That's 25 percent longer than the world record for the flight of a Frisbee, set in Sweden ninety years later. Yet the latter event generated far more fuss in the world press – at least at first – than the Wrights' accomplishment. A Dayton paper, for example, headlined its first coverage of the brothers' achievement with "Prominent Local Bicycle Merchants To Be Home For Christmas." *Scientific American* turned down an account of the event by A. I. Root, of Medina, Ohio, who then offered it to *Gleanings in Bee Culture*, where it ran as an exclusive. When North American newspapers finally did get off the mark, they generally ran the story a little straighter than some European dailies like France's *Le Pays*, where an article bubbled enthusiastically about Monsieur Wilbug Bright and his glider!

Q: What did Lorne "Gump" Worsley play for the New York Rangers?

A: Yes, he played in goal.

The Challenge

Q: What did Gladys Goodding play for the New York Rangers?

A: **The organ.** She had a long and appreciated tenure at Madison Square Garden, playing for Knicks games, too, and also played at Ebbett's Field for the Brooklyn Dodgers. At NHL games, Ms. Goodding had a special song for the visiting teams: e.g., "Pretty Red Wing" for Detroit, "Chicago" for the Blackhawks, and "Canadian Capers" for Montreal. For reasons still unexplained, the Toronto Maple Leafs were welcomed with a song called "Saskatchewan."

The Madison Square Garden that Goodding played in, the third of four Gardens, was built in 1925, right about the time the electric organ was developed. While this instrument seems especially well suited to sports arenas, it appears to be approaching its first centenary without ever garnering a single word of praise from musicologists. Granted, this august group have never commented either on two other inventions that, for some, have a measure of appeal equal to that of the electric organ, namely the electric dentist's drill and the electric chair. The drill (1908) lagged the appearance of the chair by nearly twenty years (first use: 1890 at Auburn Prison, NY), but both predate the organ.

Although the first official use of the electric chair generated a very negative official review, this did not deter Emperor Menelik II of Ethiopia, who imported three of them in the 1890s. As it turned out, the only citizen to be shocked was the emperor himself when he discovered they required a power source to perform (Ethiopia did not yet have electricity). His Excellency responded with true regal creativity by converting the chairs into imperial thrones. Waste not, want not.

Menelik died in 1913, too soon to have experimented with alternative uses for the electric organ. (They're hard to sit on, in any case.)

Q: There was a worldwide fad in the late 1970s, when it seemed that everyone was playing with a multicolored cube puzzle made up of smaller, pivoting cubes. What was this puzzle called?

A: Yes, Rubik's Cube, named after the Hungarian architect who patented the entertaining device in 1975.

The Challenge

Q: Was "Rubik" his first name or his surname?

A: **Surname.** Erno Rubik, however, liked to be called "Doctor" Rubik.

Some other "doctors" whose first names don't readily spring to mind include Dr. (Victor) Frankenstein, Dr. (Julius) No of James Bond fame, Dr. (Henry) Jekyll – his Mr. Hyde alternate was Edward – and Dr. (John Hamish) Watson. Watson is the "Elementary, my dear Watson" companion of Sherlock Holmes, who never once used the phrase in a Conan Doyle novel. Flash Gordon never said "Elementary" to his friend Dr. (Hans) Zharkov, nor did anyone speak that way to Dr. Strangelove or to Dr. Who, neither of whom had first names. Dr. Seuss, who, like Dr. Rubik, is real, was Theodor Seuss Geisel. Dr. Pepper is real, too, but not a person. It's a soft drink dreamed up in 1885 in Waco, Texas, by R. S. Lazenby, who was not a doctor.

An unintended outcome of the cube fad was the addition of "Rubik's Thumb" to the catalog of human complaints. It's an affliction in the same medical category as "Jogger's Kidney," which should be self-evident, and "Jogger's Nipple," which is potentially more interesting. There's also "Jeans Folliculitis," an irritation of the hair follicles on the upper thigh, caused by tight jeans, and as well, the relatively uncommon "Musher's Knee," uncommon because it is generally visited only upon dogsled drivers who overtrain.

Lest you think I am making these up, check the *New England Journal of Medicine*. Start with a 1978 article which describes how eating a bowl of wonton soup caused a patient to have a relapse of Kwok's Disease. Kwok's, apparently caused by overdoses of MSG, is also known as Chinese Restaurant Syndrome.

23

Q: Since 1910, Hollywood has averaged over ten releases a year on sport subjects. Now, even if you have never seen Rocky Balboa perform, you should know what sport has shown up most frequently in the movies.

A: Yes, boxing. By far.

The Challenge

Q: What sport comes in at number two?

A: **Horse racing,** two to one over baseball (which is fifth behind football and auto racing) and six to one over golf (in ninth place, right behind wrestling).

The one-two punch, so to speak, of boxing and horse racing is not surprising given that these two activities were widely popular long before baseball or golf. The first sports-dedicated periodical in North America was *The American Turf Register and Sporting Magazine*, launched in 1829. It catered to horse owners and betting enthusiasts, with only the odd mention of other sports. By 1876, the year sportswriter Henry Chadwick helped create the National (baseball) League, baseball had zoomed from nowhere into the top ten in audience appeal, but that was only in North America. Internationally, the sport that occupied the most interest, at least as far as organized competitions were concerned, was *rowing*, with the big competitors being Canada, Britain, Australia, the U.S.A., and France.

Sport historians today are amazed that races on the Thames, and the St. Lawrence, and the Hudson, drew huge crowds in the nineteenth century, especially since large chunks of the audience were often unable to see the finish and for obvious reasons could not rely on "live" reporting. But then, even after live radio broadcasts made it unnecessary to go to the river at all, boat race aficionados were still dealt a short hand on occasion, the most famous example coming from veteran BBC announcer John Snagge during the stretch at the annual Oxford–Cambridge race in 1949: "Oxford are ahead! (. . . pause . . .) No! Cambridge are ahead! (. . . pause . . .) I don't know who's ahead! (. . . pause . . .) But it's either Oxford or Cambridge!"

Rowing is eleventh on the movie list, tied with skiing and polo, all well ahead of kick-boxing, bowling, and cockfighting.

Q: Most historians agree that a car driven on the streets of Munich, Germany, in 1886 was the world's first motorcar. Who built this car?

A: Sure, Karl Benz (not to be confused with another German, Melitta Bentz – no relation – who came up with the paper coffee filter some twenty years later).

The Challenge

Q: Who built the first motorcycle?

A: **Gottleib Daimler.** His company joined with Benz's in 1926 to form Daimler-Benz. (For your notebook: Mercedes, of the Mercedes-Benz we all know, was a daughter of popular Austrian racing driver Emil Jellinek, who drove Daimler cars he nicknamed "Mercedes." The name is her only contribution to the car.)

Daimler's invention was a wooden bicycle with an internal combustion engine. It was started by the running push method, which made it slightly more sophisticated – not to mention safer – than some competing models that appeared soon after. These contraptions were started by heating the gas line with an open flame. Such delicate operations did not deter enthusiasts, it seems, for motorcycles soon became popular. (First commercial production: Munich, 1894; first distance race: Paris, 1896; first fatality: Exeter, England, 1899; first military use: South Africa, 1900.) Not until after World War II did motorcycle "gangs" begin to form – in California (where else?) – usually adopting names that gave a strong indication of the members' worldview. The Pissed-Off Bastards of Bloomington, which later evolved into the Hell's Angels, is a prime example.

In December 1941, an Allied infantryman driving a captured Daimler auto in the Libyan Desert must have had the Hell's Angels' style in mind when he saved himself and three officers during the chaos of a retreat. One of General Rommel's officers, an adjutant no less, spotted the car, caught up to it on a motorcycle (yes, a Daimler), and began shouting, first in German, then in Italian. The driver, an Australian, shook his fist and shouted back, "Piss off, mate," at the German field officer. And he did. (Style works.)

25

Q: The brand name of a popular little round candy with a chocolate center comes right out of the middle of the alphabet — twice. What is that brand name?

A: Sure, M&M's. They hit the market in 1941.

The Challenge

Q: What does M&M stand for?

A: **Mars and Merrie,** the surnames of the co-developers. Richard Hellman went the same route in 1912 when he decided to widen the customer base for the mayonnaise his delicatessen customers liked so much. Podiatrist William Scholl and chemist Earl Tupper did, too as did Henry Ford, Ransom Olds, and host of others, including the likes of Walter Chrysler (who organized his own company after being president of the firm David Buick started). And it seems that when a developer's surname won't do, there are always possibilities inside the family. For example, in 1896, Leo Hirschfield named a new candy roll after a daughter, Clara, whom he called "Tootsie."

Sometimes it's the neighborhood that has special appeal. When Sir Marcus Sandys returned to his estate in the shire of Worcester after service in Bengal, he brought back a tangy sauce and asked two chemists, John Lea and William Perrins, to make bottles of it for his friends. He let Lea and Perrins sell it publicly as Worcester Sauce, and soon after, it crossed the Atlantic (with "shire" attached). Often, a product name is the result of "feel." Coco Chanel considered the number five lucky. Häagen-Dazs doesn't mean anything, but the developer liked its sound. George Eastman felt that way about "Kodak" (which has no meaning either). Then there's simple coincidence. When a customer told George Bunting, "Your Bunting's Sunburn Remedy sure knocked out my eczema!" the salve became Noczema.

Not that the active search method can't work too. In 1905, Lunsford Richardson was doing well enough with Richardson's Croup and Pneumonia Cure Salve, but when he jazzed up the name to Vick's VapoRub, sales really took off.

26

Q: Irving Berlin wrote some 1,500 songs, one of the most famous being "White Christmas." He wrote another very popular one for Easter. What song is that?

A: Yes, "Easter Parade."

The Challenge

Q: What did Berlin write for Thanksgiving?

A: **"I Have So Much to Be Thankful For."** Not a barnburner as it turned out, but then, neither were "Yiddle on Your Fiddle," "I Say It's Spinach," and "It Gets Lonely in the White House." Still, the hits from a man who used only the black keys on the piano because he never learned to read music, far outnumber the bombs.

Far shakier in the Thanksgiving legend category is the belief that the Mayflower pilgrims were first off the mark with the idea. The fact is, their efforts lagged those of Samuel de Champlain, in Nova Scotia, by several decades. In the autumn of 1605, Champlain and his colonists created a society called *L'Ordre de bon temps* to celebrate and give thanks. Not only did they party every night, they remembered to bring the wine (for which they built North America's first wine cellar, recently uncovered at Port Royal, N.S.). Average consumption might have been a bit steep by pilgrim standards. Records show that over that first winter, it worked out to 250 bottles a head! They ate well, too. The colonists built a trout farm, and used its resources for *chaudière* (chowder). The Micmac people taught them how to make a bean and corn mix called *succotash*, and, long before the pilgrims named Cape Cod Bay, Champlain's party had gone there to scoop oysters for their *hors d'oeuvres*. Obviously, the *real* first Thanksgiving had class.

Like Irving Berlin, these newcomers to North America had much to be thankful for, but so did another immigrant, Helmy Kresa, Irving's transcriber, manager, and good friend. When he first came to America, Kresa, a music arranger, had to work as a milkman. Thankfully, the Berlin home was on his route.

27

Q: Unlike his father, Charles I, who was somewhat of a moral terrorist, this English king was as randy as can be. Over his reign, he openly acknowledged no fewer than thirteen mistresses, the best known being his favorite, Nell Gwynn. Which Stuart king was this?

A: Indeed, Charles II.

The Challenge

Q: Nell Gwynn called him Charles III. Why?

A: **Before she took on the royal responsibility, Nell had had two other lovers named Charles.** It probably was not Nell's idea — maybe not even Charles II's — but with his reign came a heightened interest in family planning and safe sex. A variety of condoms were available at the time. One popular type was the "French bladder" (later to be euphemized to "letter"), made from the stomach membrane of a sheep. Another, developed by Italian anatomist Gabriel Fallopia about a century before, was made of linen soaked in, among other things, rum. Charles's subjects, however, being less well heeled, usually did their family planning with inexpensive folk remedies. One of these, which originated in ancient Egypt but was current in Restoration England, was the belief that conception could be prevented, or at least deferred, by applying a mixture of honey, ale, and crocodile dung (dried and powdered) to the vital areas immediately prior to engagement. The difficulty of obtaining crocodile dung, especially in moments of passion, was surmounted by turning to alternatives, chicken excrement being the hands-on favorite. Regrettably, data to support the efficacy of this method are very slim — for both crocodile dung and the chicken substitute.

It's not known whether Charles II used family planning techniques at home, for although he made specific and traceable contributions to England's population, he left the throne without a successor when he died in 1685. There is a hint, however, in a letter to the duke of Clarendon. After traveling to meet his arranged bride, Princess Catherine of Portugal, Charles wrote of his relief at not having to perform right away because he was tired. Which could well be history's first documented "Not tonight, dear" by a royal male with thirteen mistresses.

28

Q: Charles Deville Wells: he's the gambler who allegedly broke the bank so impressively that his achievement is celebrated in a song, "The Man Who Broke the Bank at . . ." At where?

A: Right, at Monte Carlo. He did it in 1891, but it wasn't a bank, it was a casino. And he didn't break it. He didn't even dent it. Still, over three days, he had one heck of a run.

The Challenge

Q: What game was he playing?

A: Roulette. Wells, an Englishman, began with a stake of £400, and increased it to £40,000. Hardly worth writing a song about, but better than losing! *And*, he quit while he was ahead! Most casinos would not permit Wells's method today. He bet on both red and black, and when he lost, simply doubled the bet next time.

One gambler who might have come closer to breaking the bank made his stand at the Desert Inn in Las Vegas in June 1950. Here, he made an incredible twenty-eight successive passes at the craps table and, had he let his winnings ride, would have rung up $300 million – in 1950 dollars! As it was, this anonymous low roller bet only two dollars on each throw, and won a total of $750.

The odds of making twenty-eight passes in a row in craps are about one in a hundred million. Math types enjoy doing these calculations, but none have volunteered any risk factor percentages in the case of Doreen Burley of England, who for thirty years regularly dusted and polished a live bomb that she'd snapped up at a boutique in Bradford and kept on display in her sitting room. (She admitted to having a real fondness for brass.) Nor have said mathpersons been inclined to offer odds on the likelihood of a visitor, one day in March 1988, being expert enough to recognize Doreen's prized *objet d'art* for what it was! On the other hand, experts assure us that in a typical six-number lottery, the odds of winning a decent jackpot are about one in twenty million. The Decoursey family of Prince Edward Island has done that twice. In between wins, their house was struck by lightning. Only once though.

Q: Baseball and cricket share many features. Both are team sports (cricket, eleven a side; baseball, nine). Both have a thrower to initiate play (cricket, the bowler; baseball, the pitcher), and both have fielders. Both have a focus-of-play area (cricket, the wickets; baseball, home plate), and both use a bat and a ball. What is the ball called in cricket?

A: Yes, a ball.

The Challenge

Q: What is the bat called in cricket?

A. **A bat.** Sharing the designation "bat," but less prone to being grabbed spontaneously by the handle, are night-flying mammals of the order Chiroptera. These creatures distinguish themselves by, among other things, sleeping upside down during the daylight hours, a behavior which leads naturally to an assessment of Millard Fillmore, thirteenth president of the United States (1850–53). Although Fillmore is often described as marginally less active than members of the order Chiroptera, despite remaining more or less right side up during the day, this reputation ignores his role in settling a bat-poop dispute between the U.S. and Peru in 1852. American businessmen had run into a snag developing the huge bat and seagull guano deposits in that South American country, and it was this neglected president who stepped into the matter.

Fillmore was served a bowl of soup on his deathbed, a gesture that enabled him to guarantee his immortality with these final words, "This nourishment is palatable." Far more memorable was the departure of Queen Caroline, wife of George II of England. "'Tis over," was her final offering, but not before she'd taken off her ring and handed it back to her husband, and then vehemently refused to allow their eldest son, Fretz (Frederick), to come and say goodbye. She hated Fretz even more than she hated George, and commented to her physician that one consolation of dying was that she would "never see that monster again." If there is an afterlife, then Fretz had the last laugh, for only weeks later he joined his mother on the other side after being struck on the head by a cricket ball.

30

Q: In 1939, Robert May wrote a poem for the Montgomery Ward department store chain to use as a Christmas promotion. The poem is a narrative about a little reindeer whose shiny nose bailed out Santa one foggy Christmas Eve, and everyone knows this reindeer's name. What is it?

A: Indeed, Rudolph, a name suggested by May's four-year-old daughter.

The Challenge

Q: What had May wanted to call him?

A: **Rollo.** The poo-bahs at Montgomery Ward nixed "Rollo," so he tried "Randolph," but they didn't like that either. Fortunately, May had the wisdom to discuss the matter with his little girl. "Rudolph the Red-Nosed Reindeer" was a success as a poem, but became a megahit when set to music. It was cowboy singer Gene Autry's biggest success (even bigger than his other macho songs like "Frosty the Snowman" and "Here Comes Peter Cottontail").

While Rudolph's red nose is admittedly a novel feature on a reindeer, the list of proboscidic anomalies among humans is actually quite extensive. A namesake, for example, Rudolf I of Hapsburg (1218–91), had a nose so large that no court painter had the nerve to be accurate. The great Michelangelo was so solidly punched out as a kid that, in the words of a contemporary, "his forehead almost overhangs the nose." Then there's gunslinger Doc Halliday's mistress, "Big-Nose Kate" (Elder), and Englishman Thomas Wedders, who took his 7.5-inch (19-cm) nose on tour in the 1750s. In Istanbul, an intriguing sequence of nasal history goes thus: A.D. 695, Leontius I overthrows Justinian II and cuts off his nose; 698, Tiberius III overthrows Leontius and cuts off his nose; 705, Justinian overthrows Tiberius and, lest proboscidectomies become a tradition, executes him – and Leontius.

Finally, as though to hint at psychic insight on the part of May's daughter, my nasal story comes full circle with astronomer Tycho Brahe (1546–1601), who lost his nose in a duel at age twenty and wore a gold prosthesis. Despite his brilliant scientific achievements, Brahe ran afoul of his chief sponsor, the king of Denmark, and left in a huff for Prague, where he took up residence with the emperor. Whose name was Rudolph.

31

Q: What legendary Swiss patriot reputedly used a crossbow to shoot an apple off his son's head?

A: Sure, William Tell. According to the story, Tell was required by a tyrannical Austrian governor to shoot at the apple from eighty paces. As everyone knows, Tell shot straight. He then shot the governor.

The Challenge

Q: What was the son's name?

A: **Walter.** You probably should get points, however, if you answered "No name at all," for despite fierce insistence — especially from the Swiss bureau of tourism — and exhibits of alleged Tell artifacts, there's no certainty that William Tell (or Walter, for that matter) ever existed. A chronicle of 1482 is credited with first mention of the story, placing the event in the year 1296. The classic form of the legend appeared in 1735 and gives the date as 1307. However, it was an 1804 play, *Wilhelm Tell* by Friedrich von Schiller, that really established the story internationally. In his very popular drama, Schiller called the son Walter.

Gioacchino Rossini gave the legend a musical boost in 1829, although his opera is known more for its overture than anything else. Even the overture owes most of its fame to WXYZ Radio in Detroit. In 1933, the station began to use it as theme music to introduce the Lone Ranger and "his faithful Indian companion, Tonto." The Lone Ranger's horse, Silver, became almost as well known as its rider. Tonto's horse, on the other hand, had a number of names. The writers tried "White Feller" and "Paint" before finally settling on "Scout." "Walter" was never considered.

Incidentally, it's probably not a good idea to dispute the truth of the Tell legend when you're in Switzerland. In the eighteenth century, one Uriel Freudenberger was sentenced to be burned alive by the Canton of Uri for publishing his opinion that the legend is of Danish origin. In fact, it appears not only in Danish but also in Norse, Finnish, English, and Russian folklore.

32

Q: The highest temperature ever recorded *in shade* is 136.4°F (58.0°C). The lowest is –128.6°F (–89.2°C). One of these readings is from Vostok; the other is from Al'Azîzîyah. Just from the look of the words, it should be fairly simple to guess which location was the high, and which the low.

A: Yes, the low reading was taken at Vostok and the high at Al'Azîzîyah.

The Challenge

Q: Al'Azîzîyah is in Libya. What's your best guess for Vostok?

A. **It's in Antarctica.** For some, the sound of "Vostok" suggests Siberia, which is not quite as cold but has the coldest permanently inhabited spot on Earth: the town of Oymyalon (pop. 4,000), where temperatures (*without* the windchill) can drop below -94°F (-70°C). This Vostok, however, is a research and weather observation site in Antarctica, our planet's fifth-largest continent.

Antarctica has 9.3 percent of Earth's land surface, and owns several bottom-end distinctions other than the lowest recorded temperature. It includes the lowest spot on any continent, the Bently Subglacial Trench, at 1.6 miles (2.5 km) below sea level (the next-lowest spot, the Dead Sea, between Israel and Jordan, is only a quarter of a mile [0.4 km] down), and it gets the least sunshine. The South Pole has 182 zero-sunshine days per year; by comparison, the North Pole has 176. Antarctica has the world's lowest birthrate — despite the cold and the poor TV reception — and the lowest number of beaches officially designated for topless sunbathing. On the other hand, it has active volcanoes, the most southerly being Mount Erebus, discovered in 1841 and first climbed in 1908 — neither of which events caused it to erupt. Also noteworthy is that Antarctica produces the world's largest icebergs, the biggest of which is larger than many countries, and it's still afloat in the South Pacific. First measured in 1956, it stretches 208 mi. x 60 mi. (335 km x 97 km). That's bigger than Belgium.

The Vostok research station has no permanent population. Neither does Vostok Atoll, part of the chain making up the Republic of Kiribati. Both are in the Pacific but they are not likely to be confused, since the atoll's mean temperature, 83°F (28.3°C) in January, drops all the way to 82°F (27.8°C) in July.

33

Q: In the latter part of the twentieth century, aggressive free-lance photographers acquired a less than complimentary title, *paparazzi*. What language contributed this word?

A: Yes, Italian.

The Challenge

Q: What does *paparazzi* mean?

A: Mosquitoes. A clever metaphor which describes the photographers' habit of swarming their subjects.

The world's 1,500 species of mosquito swarm polar bears in Greenland, jaguars in Mexico, snakes in Vietnam, and people the world over. The journals of North America's first explorers curse them. Even missionaries had trouble accepting them as God's creatures. That's not surprising. Mosquitoes can actually drain a human's blood supply. They even bite fish!

Their reputation has stimulated a great deal of study by entomologists. We know that only female mosquitoes bite, that most species have forty-seven teeth, and that if you are fair-skinned, blonde, and eat garlic, they will see you as a preferred source of food. Information like this tends to place mosquitoes even lower on the scale of appreciation than cockroaches, but this may be solely the consequence of scientists' failure to disseminate crucial information about the latter beasties. Once the world becomes more generally aware that cockroaches average four farts an hour, and continue releasing methane for eighteen hours after death, it's possible their position on the scale may be re-evaluated — along with some hitherto neglected extermination research. In 1972, electric guitarist Robert Brown reported his discovery that extremely high-pitched riffs at maximum volume will actually kill cockroaches. (But not mosquitoes, although Brown also reported what may be an unintended side benefit: during the subsequent experimentation, a family of rats abandoned his basement.)

Since audiences at rock concerts rarely complain about cockroaches, Brown's report may merit further investigation. This is not likely to be carried out in Vietnam, where it is considered bad luck to kill a cockroach. That alone may explain why there are so few rock concerts in Hanoi.

34

Q: "The best laid schemes o' mice and men / Gang aft a-gley." This line in "To a Mouse" by Scotland's national poet gave John Steinbeck the title for a prize-winning novel. Who was the poet?

A: Indeed, Robert Burns (1759–96).

The Challenge

Q: What does the line mean?

A: **The best laid plans of mice and men often go wrong.** Burns wrote the poem after inadvertently ploughing up a mouse's nest.

Few luminaries have ever proven this admonition more effectively than the dean of Hereford, the Reverend Doctor Price, in 1593. To mark special holy days, it was customary for His Eminence to lead a procession through the city, ending at the cathedral, where further ceremonies were then held. When the feast day of the cathedral's patron saint came around in '93, the usual parade was laid on, with Dean Price primed to walk at the head as was his wont. But this year, at the last moment, he decided to break with tradition. Rather than proceed afoot as the common clergy did, a position that would put him at eye – and nose – level with the unwashed masses, the good reverend determined that he should ride a horse. From such a lofty position, his reasoning went, everyone in his flock would be more certain to see him offering inspirational leadership by reading from his prayer book en route.

A sensible enough plan on the surface, except that the white mare chosen for her docility and experience in parade venues also happened to be in heat. Such an opportunity, along with the stimulus of the event, was too much for a young stallion positioned along the route. He threw his rider, jumped the mare, and performed with great enthusiasm, entirely uninhibited by the struggles of the dean trapped beneath him.

While the chronicle records that Dean Price held on to his prayer book throughout, it does not report whether he was able to do much reading. To my knowledge, there were no mice in the procession.

35

Q: Major events in aviation (rise and descent category): although others had tried before them, the Montgolfier brothers, Joseph and Jacques, were first to get one of these into the air, and then down again (in 1783). What was it?

A: Right, a hot-air balloon.

The Challenge

Q: Major events in aviation (descent only category): in 1797, André-Jacques Garnerin used a Montgolfier balloon to get up, and then became the first to come down this way. How?

A: Using a parachute. He landed without injury, but success is relative. His 'chute was an umbrella-like design with no vent, and oscillated so wildly that by touchdown, Monsieur Garnerin was violently airsick and threw up on the cheering crowd below him. Although he was careful to vent his parachute for the next jump a few days later, this time the crowd gave him an exceptionally large landing area. Despite this experience, for his first jump in England (in 1802, over London), he went back to the no-vent model and reprised the crowd surprise of his first trip!

Garnerin's behavior on this occasion may have been a consequence of haste and forgetfulness, or possibly anglophobia. Either way, it may have generated a negative attitude toward parachutes in England, for throughout World War I, British pilots tended not to use them. Their choice was not entirely irrational, given the experience of Hans Weimer of the German Air Service, who made history's first recorded use of a parachute during combat (Belgium, April 1918). Weimer bailed out of his Albatross DVa over the British trenches and was shot twenty-seven times before hitting the ground.

Aficionados of ballooning improperly credit the Montgolfiers as the first balloonists. They were the designer/manufacturers, but the first passengers (in September 1783, with Louis XVI, Marie Antoinette, and Benjamin Franklin watching) were a rooster, a sheep, and a duck. The first humans, who went up in November, were volunteers Pilâtre de Rozier and the marquis d'Arlandes. They went up about 3,000 feet (300 m) but didn't get to enjoy the view as much as they would have liked because to stay aloft, they needed lots of hot air and were kept busy feeding wood into the stove between them.

36

Q: The musical career of William John Clifton made a giant leap forward when he switched his country and western group, the Saddlemen, to the new rock 'n' roll style and adopted a new name, the Comets. Clifton himself is known by a changed name, too. What name is that?

A: Sure, Bill Haley. The group was Bill Haley and the Comets.

The Challenge

Q: What rock 'n' roll song was the Comets' first million seller?

A: "Shake, Rattle and Roll," not "Rock Around the Clock," which was recorded at the same time (1954) but didn't capture very much attention until the following year when it was used in a movie, *The Blackboard Jungle*. "Rock Around the Clock" in the opening sequence was blamed for the smash-up of theaters as teenagers leaped from the seats (*very* unusual behavior for the 1950s) to dance in the aisles. Together, the movie and song pushed rock 'n' roll into the social mainstream and made for an entire generation of terrified parents. What most parents – white ones, anyway – didn't even realize was that rock 'n' roll had long been used among black people as an idiom for partying and making love. When black blues singer Trixie Smith recorded "My Daddy Rocks Me (with One Steady Roll)," for example, in 1922, she wasn't talking cradle techniques.

"Rock Around the Clock," written by James E. Myers, a.k.a. Jimmy DeKnight, has topped 100 million in sales, has been recorded by artists as diverse as the Beatles and Mae West, and is still seen as the anthem of the genre. But it was certainly not a rock 'n' roll first. Duke Ellington had "Rockin' in Rhythm" for RCA Victor in 1931. Wynonie Harris's "Good Rockin' Tonight" was a hit in 1948. And fans, when asked to pick the first truly rock 'n' roll song, usually point to a song from 1951, "Rocket 88" by Jackie Brenston and Ike Turner (Tina's 'ex').

Bill Haley freely admitted his debt to British astronomer Edmund Halley (of Halley's Comet). Interestingly, although Haley's career went flat in North America after "Rock Around the Clock," his reappearance in England always got attention.

37

Q: On June 1, 1813, off the coast of Boston, U.S. Admiral James Lawrence lay dying on the deck of USS *Chesapeake* and told his officers, "Don't give up the . . ." The what?

A: Yes, the ship. (What Lawrence actually said was, "Tell the men to fire faster and not to give up the ship; fight her till she sinks.")

The Challenge

Q: Did they give up the ship?

A: **Yes.** The *Chesapeake* was captured by HMS *Shannon* and towed to Halifax.

This bell-ringing phrase is by no means the only piece of military history to have undergone convenient fudging. Teddy Roosevelt's Rough Riders never "charged" up San Juan Hill in 1898. First of all, it was *Kettle* Hill, and they *walked* up because their horses hadn't yet arrived in Cuba! Then there's the famous "Don't fire until you see the whites of their eyes," credited to William Prescott at the battle of Bunker Hill, 1775 (fought on *Breed's* Hill — it never ends!). This one was lifted either from Prince Charles of Prussia, who used it in 1745, or possibly from Frederick the Great, who said it a decade later. In 1864, in Georgia, General William Sherman allegedly signaled "Hold the fort" to fellow general John Murray Corse. The real message was "Hold out; relief is coming." (Sherman, who had a reputation for court-martialing what he called "dirty newspaper scribblers who have the impudence of Satan," is also the reported author of "War is hell," but swore he had no memory of ever saying that.)

For the most part, the media are blamed for truth-twisting, along with a public eager for words that stick in the mind. That might explain why former president Harry Truman was so crystal clear when he explained to reporters why he fired General Douglas MacArthur: "I didn't fire him because he was a dumb son of a bitch, although he was. But that's not against the law for generals." Truman went on, "If it was, half to three-quarters of them would be in jail."

38

Q: In 1893, at Louisville Experimental Kindergarten in Kentucky, teachers Mildred and Patty Hill wrote a simple little song that is better known and more frequently sung than the national anthem. What is the title of the song?

A: Indeed, "Happy Birthday to You."

The Challenge

Q: What title did Mildred and Patty give it?

A: **"Good Morning to All."** It was used as a morning welcome in the school, and was published, in 1893, under copyright.

In 1924, it appeared – unauthorized – in a songbook edited by Robert Coleman, who had altered the lyrics of the second verse to say "Happy birthday to you." When the song showed up in Irving Berlin's musical *As Thousands Cheer* in 1934, a third Hill sister, Jessica, took the copyright issue to court and won. People were flabbergasted to learn that the song was not public property, not least Western Union, which promptly dropped it as a singing telegram. *As Thousands Cheer* dropped it, too. A few years later, Helen Hayes was reduced to speaking it in the Broadway play *Happy Birthday* so producers could avoid royalty payments. However, at family parties you can still sing it without much legal risk, under a copyright loophole usually referred to as "one-time personal use."

This escape clause would have been very important in the household of Augustus the Strong, king of Poland from 1697 to 1706, then again from 1710 to 1733. Augustus is reported to have fathered over 300 children while he was king, which may explain why he took the four years off. Regrettably, since the precise number of Augustus's offspring is uncertain, the recording of their birthdates is equally unreliable, so we don't know if any of them celebrated on the same day. Statistically, it's almost certain they did. Demographers have established that on any given day, more than ten million people on our planet are having a birthday.

For horror-movie buffs: Vincent Price and Peter Cushing were born on May 27. Christopher Lee arrived May 26, but it's known that his mother was always in a rush.

39

Q: In the words of Lord Acton, "Power tends to corrupt and absolute power corrupts . . ." What's the rest of it?

A: Right, "absolutely."

The Challenge

Q: Whose absolute power was His Lordship commenting on?

A: **The pope's,** specifically, the doctrine of papal infallibility proclaimed by the Vatican Council of 1869–79.

Lord Acton (John Emerich Edward Dalberg-Acton, first baron Acton) was Regius Professor of Modern History at Cambridge, and a liberal Roman Catholic critical of papal power and especially of the lock that Italian cardinals seemed to have on the papacy. When Acton made his now-famous statement in 1887, Italians had sat in the papal chair for 365 years in a row – ever since 1523, the year that Pope Adrian VI of the Netherlands said that all evils in the Church proceeded from the Roman Curia (the Vatican's inner circle and power group). On another occasion Adrian observed, "In truth, many Roman Pontiffs were heretics." Quite possibly, comments like these were enough to squelch any leanings toward ethnic diversity among those in the back rooms.

For some reason the Adrians seem to stick out. Adrian II (867–72), the last married pope, refused to renounce his wife and family as he was expected to. The first Adrian (772–95) lived to 103. He granted Charlemagne the right to appoint popes. In 1276, Adrian V made pope in a single leap, without ever having been a bishop or even a priest. But he lasted only six weeks. (A tough year, 1286: there were *four* popes!) The only English pope was Adrian IV (1154–59), who was not overly fond of his Italian colleagues but choked on a fly in his drink and died before he could really lock horns.

Adrian VI was the last Adrian. Clement XIV abolished papal toe-kissing in 1773. He was the last Clement.

40

Q: An animal with two feet is called a biped. Using the same classification method, what do we call an animal with four feet?

A: Yes, a quadruped.

The Challenge

Q: What is a pinniped?

A. **An animal with fin-like flippers,** such as the seal or walrus.

Dogs are quadrupeds; actually, *digitigrade* quadrupeds, meaning they walk on their toes. Among the better-known digitigrade quadruped canines, thanks to Hollywood, are Lassie (the first of whom, to settle arguments once and for all, was male) and Rin Tin Tin. Less well known is an Alsatian named Gus who starred in *Won Ton Ton, the Dog Who Saved Hollywood.* At the premiere, 100 of the 576 first-nighters were dogs. The 476 bipeds, most of whom were human, did not offer comment later as to how much the quadrupeds enjoyed the movie. In any case, the filmmakers were sued by the Rin Tin Tin estate for allegedly stealing the story of "Rinty's" life, and the movie was allowed to quietly fade away.

Rin Tin Tin Jr., although he may have been more deserving of legal action, managed to escape unscathed. In his first successful movie, *The Canine Detective* (1936), RTT Jr. displayed his powers as man's best friend by capturing an entire group of robbers on his own. Shortly after the movie's release, and miles from the set, he managed to maintain a blissful, uninterrupted sleep at the home of his master, Lee Duncan, while a break-and-enter team cleaned it out. Yet Junior's sin of neglect pales in comparison to a favorite case among British barristers, namely that of Caliph, a Great Dane, whose fate was being determined in a court case because he had bitten a neighbor. While the lawyers were engaged in hot debate before the bench, Caliph bit the judge.

41

Q: This singer's first record, cut in 1956, was *Blue Days, Black Nights* and it did nothing for his career. The second, *Modern Don Juan*, did even less. But after he led his band through *That'll Be the Day* in 1957, he became a musical icon. Who was the singer?

A: Sure, Buddy Holly.

The Challenge

Q: What was the band?

A♪. The Crickets. Holly and the Crickets had four more hits together in quick succession before Holly split. Only two months later, on February 3, 1959, he died in the plane crash that also killed Richie Valens and one-hit wonder J. P. Richardson, better known as the Big Bopper.

Musicologists regard Buddy Holly and the Crickets as fundamental shapers of the rock 'n' roll idiom. Only the great Chuck Berry may have been more important. Meteorologists, on the other hand, generally fail to acknowledge the contribution of crickets to weather forecasting, even though it has been scientifically established that the chirps of a cricket can be used to get temperature readings at least as accurate as those from the average household wall thermometer. To do it in Celsius, you count the number of chirps in fifteen seconds. Call that x. Divide x by 2 to get y. Now add x and y to get z, and then simply add 6 to z and you have the temperature. Fahrenheit is easier: it's the number of chirps in fifteen seconds plus 40. Needless to say, you need a cricket, which may be an important reason why the procedure is not taught in Arctic survival courses.

By peeking into the appropriate areas, entomologists have determined that only the male cricket chirps, and like the glowworm, he generally does it for sex. But whereas a glowworm can usually tell right away whether the wine and soft music is paying off – excited females emit a strong light pulse every 2.1 seconds on average – the male cricket must keep sawing away. Contrary to popular belief, by the way, rubbing the wings together, not the legs, produces the come-on sound. It's rock 'n' roll singers who use the legs.

42

Q: Where does John Brown's body "lie a-molderin'"?

A: Yes, "in the grave."

The Challenge

Q: Where's the grave?

A: **Lake Placid, New York,** at John Brown Farm State Historic Site. Brown's headstone is from his grandfather's grave in Ohio – one of his pre-gallows requests. A relatively tame burial arrangement compared to that of evangelist Aimee Semple McPherson, founder of the Church of the Foursquare Gospel. She had a telephone installed in her coffin before she passed on in 1944.

McPherson, like John Brown, was interred in the traditional, horizontal, face-up style. Not so for French premier Georges Clemenceau (d. 1929); he stands upright, facing Germany. Shakespeare's contemporary Ben Jonson also departed from custom. When he died in 1637, there wasn't quite enough space in Westminster Abbey's Poets' Corner for a conventional stretch, so he's in a sitting position. Still, neither of these has a patch on Mogul emperor Khan Jahan (a.k.a. Shah Jahan; he had the Taj Mahal built). When this worthy met his eternal reward in 1666, a special conical tomb was constructed above ground, and he was placed in it – upright – with one hand sticking out so devoted subjects could maintain contact.

Each of the above interees became *defunctus officio* too soon to have joined the Society for Perpendicular Interment, founded in Melbourne, Australia, but then, they may not have been all that keen anyway, since the society recommends cardboard coffins. Cardboard might have made a difference in 1675 in Basingstoke, England, when the good citizens buried a woman alive. Although they had acted in good faith, and did in fact dig her up once their collective "was she, or wasn't she?" doubt became strong enough (they were too late), the sheriff of Hampshire was not impressed, and fined the town £100. Clearly, Basingstoke is no place to molder.

43

Q: "Bibbidi-Bobbidi-Boo" was nominated for best song at the 1950 Oscars. "Zip-A-Dee-Doo-Dah" was nominated for 1947. What studio produced the movies that gave us these unusually titled songs?

A: Sure, Walt Disney Productions.

The Challenge

Q: Only one of the songs was an Oscar winner. Which one?

♫ **"Zip-A-Dee-Doo-Dah,"** from *Song of the South.* "Bibbidi-Bobbidi-Boo," from *Cinderella*, performed on the big night by Dean Martin and Jerry Lewis, lost out to "Mona Lisa" from *Captain Carey, USA.* A few years earlier, Disney Studios had another win-lose combination with "When You Wish Upon a Star" from *Pinocchio* (1940) and "Love Is a Song" from *Bambi* (1942; it lost to "White Christmas").

Cartooned animal characters in Disney productions are usually very authentic in movement and behavior, something Walt always insisted on. While *Bambi* was in production, for example, animators had two live fawns from Maine (named Bambi and Faline) to guide them. Walt also brought in a deer carcass for dissection and anatomy lessons. At the same time, the studio went to great lengths to make the characters anthropomorphic (human-like), notwithstanding the fact that Mickey Mouse has a thumb and three fingers on each hand. However, with the stories themselves, Disney was a lot more freewheeling. The original *Cinderella*, written by Charles Perrault around 1700, had a slipper made of fur, and the last-minute transformations before the ball were made by an old hag. In the original *Pinocchio*, by Carlo Lorenzi, published in 1881, the little puppet is an out and out brat who fidgets during Jiminy Cricket's advice, then squashes him and goes on to become a genuine juvenile delinquent.

That little twist may have had resonance with eleven short people Disney hired to dance and sing outside the theater on the day of the *Pinocchio* premiere. After a boring morning, they got completely plastered at lunch and by mid-afternoon were cavorting naked atop the marquee. A tractable troupe, nevertheless: too smashed to dress themselves, they allowed police to carry them off in pillowcases.

Q: Sports names that end in "o": *Joe DiMaggio*. In what sport did he excel?

A: Yes, baseball.

The Challenge

Q: Sports names that end in "o": *Guy Lombardo*. In what sport did he excel?

A: **Speedboat racing.** Yes, this is the same Guy Lombardo whose orchestra created the "sweetest music this side of heaven" and who for thirty-three years had a lock on New Year's Eve celebrations in North America, playing "Auld Lang Syne" at midnight in New York. But he didn't stop there; Lombardo was also an avid boat racer. In 1946, he won the sport's Gold Cup in a hydroplane called *Tempo VI*. With the same machine he took the President's Cup and the National Sweeps three times, setting several world records in the process.

Nineteen forty-six saw another speed record that has yet to be toppled, this time in boxing. On September 23, in Lewiston, Maine, Al Couture knocked out Ralph Walton at 10.5 seconds of the first round. And that includes the 10-second count! Couture, a notoriously aggressive opener, sprang across the ring at the opening bell. Walton, equally notorious for being a slow starter, was still putting in his mouth guard when the punch landed. Just a few years later and down the coast at Providence, Rhode Island, professional wrestler Stanley Pinto put the shortest-ever wrestling contest into the books, by pinning himself to the mat (this was in a *straight* match). He was stretching on the ropes as the bell rang, and got tangled up with his shoulders pressed long enough for the referee to count him out. Pinto's appeal was denied.

Guy Lombardo's *Tempo VI* could achieve speeds of over 140 mph (225 km/h) going against the current. To put that in perspective, the highest speed ever recorded for a racing pigeon is 110 mph (177 km/h). That was with a gale-force tailwind.

45

Q: The siege of Troy turned out badly for just about everyone involved, especially two of the women prominent in the story. One was the beautiful lady abducted by Paris. Her name?

A: Sure, Helen. She's best known as Helen of Troy, although she was really Helen of Greece, where she was married to Menelaus when Paris showed up.

The Challenge

Q: The other woman was Paris's sister. She was gifted with the ability to predict the future, and cursed in that no one would believe her warnings. Her name?

A: **Cassandra.** She had the bad luck to attract the attention of Apollo, who, in the "if it turns you on, go get it" tradition so well established by his father, Zeus, skipped right past the flowers-and-chocolates routine and wooed her with the psychic gift. When Cassandra replied, "Not tonight and not *ever!*" to his overtures, Apollo added the curse.

The prediction business has had its ups and downs since Cassandra. Take the medical faculty at the University of Paris, for example. Early in April of the year 1348, they issued this statement:

> . . . on March 20, there was a conjunction of the planets Saturn, Jupiter and Mars in the House of Aquarius. The conjunction of Saturn and Jupiter portends death and disaster. The conjunction of Mars and Jupiter portends pestilence in the air. Jupiter is warm and humid and draws up evil vapors . . . Mars is hot and dry and kindles the evil into an infective fire. We must therefore expect a terrible calamity.

Like Cassandra's fellow Trojans, the Parisians scoffed at the warning. By June, the Black Death had taken hold throughout France.

A more recent example arose on the morning of December 6, 1941. Secretary of the Navy Frank Knox asked the U.S. Navy's War Plans Division if Japan might attack. "No, Mr. Secretary," replied Admiral Turner. "They are going to hit the British. They're not ready for us yet."

Fortunately, modern science and advanced research methodology have added a greater degree of certainty to authoritative statements. Like the one made on May 16, 1975, by the World Health Organization, which announced in Geneva that "malaria has been licked." That was the day the WHO's deputy director-general, Dr. Thomas Lambo, was hospitalized. With malaria.

46

Q: In 1337, Edward III of England claimed the throne of France and thereby launched what many believe to be the longest war in history. What war?

A: Right, the Hundred Years' War.

The Challenge

Q: How long did it last?

A: **One hundred and sixteen years,** until 1453. But it wasn't really a continuous war, more a series of periodic flare-ups highlighted by major battles with pre- and post-raiding. The combatants, especially the knights, avoided fighting in bad weather, on Sundays and feast days, or if someone of major importance on either side was indisposed by something like illness or trouble at home. By these standards, a better candidate for the longest war is the *Reconquista*, the campaign in what are now Spain and Portugal to oust the Islamic Moors. That one started in 718 and ran hot and cold until the last Moorish stronghold went down at Granada in the same year that Columbus first crossed the Atlantic.

Wars tend to attract identifying names that are not always explanatory. The War of Jenkins' Ear (1739–48) was really about the Austrian succession, even though there was a Jenkins (Captain Robert) who sailed from the Caribbean back to England with his ear in a jar, just to prove the Spanish were bad guys. On the other hand, the War of the Spanish Succession was really between France on one side and England, the Netherlands, and several German states on the other. Then there's the incredibly bloody War of the Triple Alliance. The alliance members were Brazil, Argentina, and Uruguay, and they gave the war its name despite the fact that the other side, Paraguay, suffered most. In six years of fighting (1864–70), that country's population was reduced from 1,400,000 to 220,000!

If nations must fight wars, then they should follow the example of the titanic struggle of Sultan Sa'îd Khalid of Zanzibar versus the British Empire. From declaration to surrender on August 27, 1896, this war lasted thirty-eight minutes. And it doesn't have a name.

47

Q: What was Abraham Lincoln doing the night he was shot by John Wilkes Booth?

A: Sure, he was attending a play at Ford's Theater in Washington.

The Challenge

Q: What was the play?

Aᵉ **Our American Cousin,** a rather inconsequential drawing room comedy. General and Mrs. Grant were to go with the Lincolns, but Julia Grant, like many others in the Washington social whirl, avoided Mary Lincoln as much as possible and canceled out. The Lincolns were accompanied instead by Major Henry Rathbone and Clara Harris, a senator's daughter. (Major Rathbone later married Ms. Harris and then murdered her.)

In light of the obsessive security surrounding the U.S. head of state today, Lincoln's situation was tragicomic. His one official guard, an alcoholic policeman, had taken off for a drink, leaving Lincoln's coachman on guard. He passed Wilkes Booth through, believing he was an official messenger. The aftermath of the assassination was equally bizarre. Some 2,000 people were arrested; four were hanged, among them Mary Surratt, who owned the boarding house where Booth's plot was allegedly hatched. Another was George Atzerodt, who was supposed to kill Vice-President Andrew Johnson but got drunk instead. The doctor who tended Booth after his escape from the theater was given life. And since the judiciary was on a roll, the former president of the Confederacy, Jefferson Davis, was tried and convicted *in absentia*.

The nineteenth century saw the U.S. losing two presidents to assassination when President Garfield followed Lincoln only sixteen years later. Russia also lost two leaders, Czars Paul I in 1801 and Alexander II in 1881. Britain lost a prime minister in 1812, France a president in 1894, and Spain its premier three years after that.

48

Q: What number in sport is a "hat trick"?

A: Sure, three.

The Challenge

Q: What sport gave us this phrase?

A: **Cricket.** Its widest use is in hockey, but the phrase comes from a tradition in cricket wherein a bowler is awarded a hat if he takes three wickets in three consecutive balls.

Other "threes" of note: a male chimpanzee takes three seconds to complete intercourse — although he is rarely given a hat for the achievement. "Three" also figures prominently in a completely different erection: the Eiffel Tower. Its height increases by up to three inches on hot, sunny days. The largest number that can be written with three digits is nine to the ninth to the ninth power, or $9^{387420489}$. Written out, the number would be 369 million digits long, and would require about 22,000 pages of normal-sized text. Not hard to see, therefore, why research psychologists never try to teach it to chimpanzees, given their time-on-task behavior.

"Three" has had repercussions for Australia. That's how many pairs of rabbits were set loose there by animal fanciers in the middle of the nineteenth century. Although rabbits are fornicators of legendary capacity, they are not limited to this achievement alone. They are also one of nature's most prolific defecators, dropping pellets at a rate of three every half minute while awake. That works out to better than 3,000 per day per rabbit. When that production level is multiplied by Australia's millions of rabbits, it's no wonder a local term for hiking is "walkabout."

Rabbits are born bald. Hares arrive with hair (actually, *fur*, but it doesn't sound as interesting that way). Hares are also larger, have black ear tips, and are more solitary (rarely traveling in threes). The Belgian hare is a rabbit, so in its case none of these differences apply.

49

Q: In the assassination scene of Shakespeare's *Julius Caesar*, Caesar's final words are addressed to one of the conspirators. They begin, "*Et tu, . . . ?*" ("You too, . . . ?"). What conspirator is he speaking to?

A: Right, Brutus. Caesar says, "*Et tu, Brute?* Then, fall, Caesar!"

The Challenge

Q: Is that what he actually said on the Ides of March in 44 B.C.?

A. Many scholars believe the words were Greek, "Kai su, teknon!" The phrase "*Kai su*" appears in ancient mosaics and on graffiti-marked walls uncovered by archeologists and translates as an equivalent of "Screw you!" "*Teknon*" means "son" in the sense of "kid," so "Screw you, kid!" may be how Caesar gasped his last.

Somehow this jewel escaped the moralizing eye of Thomas Bowdler (1754–1825), editor of *Bowdler's Family Shakespeare* and the man credited with cleansing Shakespeare's plays of — as the title page of the 1818 edition claims — "words and expressions which cannot with propriety be read aloud in a family." It must have got by Bowdler's Victorian readers, too, for this publication eventually became a ten-volume undertaking and went through thirty printings. Most of the "bowdlerizing" was actually done by Thomas's sister Harriet (although Thomas later took on Gibbon's *History of the Decline and Fall of the Roman Empire* all on his own; and the Old Testament, too). However, it would have been unseemly to credit Harriet, for that would mean she *knew* what was dirty in order to take it out! In an era when manuals of etiquette stipulated that books by male and female authors should not even touch while standing on a shelf, the Thomas-not-Harriet decision made good business sense.

Such extreme censorship often stimulated a remarkable degree of creativity among the Victorians. William Whewell, for example, master of Trinity College, Cambridge, was escorting Queen Victoria over the river Cam, which at the time (1849) was doing duty as an open sewer. When the queen innocently inquired about the many square pieces of paper floating on the water, he replied, "Those, madam, are notices to inform visitors that the river is unfit for bathing."

50

Q: Who wrote *Riders of the Purple Sage*?

A: Right, Zane Grey. It was published by Harpers in 1912.

The Challenge

Q: Was his name really Zane?

A: **Yes,** although he was baptized *Pearl* Zane *Gray*. However, for a young man who was once a major league baseball prospect before turning to dentistry, it's no surprise the "Pearl" fell by the wayside. Why the vowel shift to "Grey" took place is uncertain. Zane's first novel, *Betty Zane* (1903) was a self-published undertaking that bombed completely, and he was forced to go back to dentistry until *Riders of the Purple Sage* enabled him to exchange his drill for a pen. Several excellent and successful novels followed *Riders*, before our hero took a short-lived stab at yet another career. He played a shark hunter in a low-budget Australian movie, *The White Death*, in 1936. Fortunately for his reputation, Zane Grey's accomplishments as an actor are about as well known as his contributions to the field of dentistry.

Another prominent "Grey" author is Grey Owl, an alleged native Canadian writer whose fame eclipsed that of Zane in the 1930s, at least outside the U.S. The British in particular were captivated by Wa-Sha-Quon-Asin (the Ojibwa version of "Grey Owl"), whom they regularly described as a "Red" Indian (thereby implying the possibility that Canadian aboriginals are born in a variety of colors!). No one seemed to find it odd that Grey Owl was allegedly half-*Apache*, a people whose home is worlds away from Canada, and it wasn't until after his death that he was discovered to be Archibald Stansfield Belaney, born in Hastings, England, in 1888.

In a world where the Douglas fir is really a pine, where there are no guinea pigs in Guinea, and where quicksand is actually *slow*, Belaney's deception was, relatively, a harmless one. Besides, how can an adventure lover lose oneself in a nature story by an author named Archibald? (Or, for that matter, in a western written by Pearl?)

51

Q: Who is Luke Skywalker's father?

A: Sure, Darth Vader, the arch-villain who went over to the "dark side."

The Challenge

Q: Who is Luke Skywalker's mother?

A: **We're never told,** not in the *Star Wars* movies, nor in the original book.

If Anna Jarvis were still around, this might not have happened. She got Mother's Day going in 1907. The day was made official in 1915, the same year Margaret Sanger was jailed for *Family Limitation*, her book on birth control. In the U.S., Canada, and Australia, Mother's Day is the second Sunday in May. In the U.K., the fourth Sunday of Lent is "Mothering Sunday." There is no Margaret Sanger day.

Generally, with the exception of items like mother of vinegar, the bacterial slime added to wine or cider to start production of vinegar, "mother" is usually used in a complimentary way, despite some of the more legendary tigers of the species like Agrippina, the mother of Nero. Notwithstanding her major commitments on Nero's behalf (e.g., she poisoned her third husband, the emperor Claudius, to get her son onto the imperial throne), Nero went to some lengths to get rid of his mom. He tried poison three times (bad choice; this was her specialty), arranged for her bedroom ceiling to collapse (the timing was off), sent her on a Mediterranean errand in a boat designed to fall apart (she swam ashore), and finally had centurions beat her to death. Nero's contemporaries, incidentally, agreed completely with his objective.

A more palatable image arises from the mother of Jesus, Mary of Nazareth, no relation, as far is known, of Mary Marcos of Nazareth, who on December 24, 1955, went into labor during a trip to Bethlehem and had a son the next day. Jordanian authorities allowed mother and child to stay on that side of the armistice line for a week – at the time, an unusual example of cooperation in the Middle East. Mothers rule!

52

Q: If *The Greatest Names in Indoor Plumbing* is ever published, it's sure to include Sir John Harrington, Alexander Cumming, and Thomas Crapper. With what indoor plumbing device are they associated?

A: Correct, the flush toilet.

The Challenge

Q: Which of them is the inventor?

A: **None of them.** Flushing goes back to the Minoans, 4,000 years ago (and *their* kids always forgot, too!).

Sir John Harrington's model (1596), often cited as first, was actually a re-invention. Having run afoul of his godmother, Elizabeth I, for selling dirty books from Italy, Harrington tried to regain favor by making his loo a royal one. It flushed well, and Her Majesty was favorably impressed even though the design allowed odor to drift back up the drainpipe. Unfortunately, Harrington ran afoul again, this time by writing a joke book about the queen's new can, and thereby derailed plumbing progress until 1775, when watchmaker Alexander Cumming came up with a device still used today: the S (for "stink") trap, which keeps water in the pipe after a flush, thus blocking smells.

Thomas Crapper was a nineteenth-century businessman with such flair that many think he was the toilet's inventor. His slogans like "Certain Flush With Easy Pull" and clever additions like aromatic seats influenced even Queen Victoria, who guaranteed his fame by granting him a contract for *thirty* loos at Sandringham Castle. But even for Crapper, it was a struggle to get the middle classes to opt for the flush, so strong was their bond with outdoor privies. A prime example: in 1852, a public lavatory (the brainchild of Samuel Peto, who built Nelson's Column in Trafalgar Square, and Henry Cole, the father of the Christmas card) was installed in London. Despite heavy advertising (three times a week in *The Times*), a pleasantly euphemistic name ("Public Waiting Rooms"), and spanking cleanliness, the lavs attracted only an average fifty-eight flushes a month and were soon closed.

53

Q: In 1956, Gamal Abdel Nasser seized the Suez Canal in Egypt, Fidel Castro landed with a small force in Cuba, and Cardinal Wyszynski left prison in Poland. What did Prince Rainier do in Monaco?

A: Right, he married Grace Kelly.

The Challenge

Q: What did Warwick Kerr do in Brazil?

A. **He let loose twenty-six swarms of killer bees.** Kerr was part of a group experimenting with the crossbreeding of native bees and a much more aggressive African strain, when a number of the research subjects escaped.

Apis mellifera scellatus is notorious not so much for the nature of its sting as for its attack. African bees, or "killer" bees as they have come to be called, sting up to sixty times a minute, in assaults that can last for hours. Since 1956, Brazilian authorities have attributed over 300 deaths to the bees. In 1973, they laid siege to part of a town (Recife), and dispersed only when set upon by asbestos-clad firemen using flame-throwers. Until the early 1990s, the bees moved slowly northward, being blamed for deaths in Central America, Mexico, and Texas, but their spread seems to have been stopped by temperate climes. Reproduction and mortality rates, too, have affected their numbers, for they face the same fates as other bees, like being eaten by birds. And then there's the matter of simply being kept busy in the search for food. (Production of a single pound [0.45 kg] of honey by a hive of domestic bees involves about four million nectar visits!)

Finally, to make the "killers" seem even less threatening, entomologists point out that despite their famed aggressiveness, these bees seem to be rather unenthusiastic breeders. Readers of Adrian Forsyth's *A Natural History of Sex* will not be surprised at this. Forsyth reports that at the end of a successful copulation with a queen bee, the testicles of a mating male (drone) explode with an audible pop. Not exactly an appealing substitute for pillow talk!

54

Q: At what famous spot on Earth did Robert E. Peary stand on April 6, 1909?

A: Yes, the North Pole.

The Challenge

Q: At what famous spot on Earth did Matthew Henson, Ootah, Seegloo, Ooqeah, and Egingwah stand on April 6, 1909?

A. **Same place.** Peary's final-dash team consisted of the four Canadian Inuit men and his longtime associate, Matthew Henson (who had been a hat salesman before he met Peary).

Because of delays, Peary didn't reach a telegraph line until September (in Labrador). He first wired Mrs. Peary that he'd reached the D.O.P. (damned old Pole) at last, and then President Taft that he had the honor, etc., etc. However, four days earlier, Taft had received a telegram from explorer Frederick A. Cook saying *he* had reached the North Pole. Although Cook's curriculum vitae contains several fraud convictions and expulsion from the Explorers' Club for falsely claiming a climb of Mount McKinley, the Cook–Peary–North Pole controversy lives on. As recently as the 1980s, a CBS television program favored Cook, suggesting that the National Geographic Society no less (a Peary sponsor) was part of a pro-Peary deception. But the weight of hard evidence is overwhelmingly on Peary's side in this fuss.

You may have heard of Matthew Henson. He was a black man and now figures prominently in American "catch-up" history. But it's unlikely that the names Ootah, Seegloo, Ooqeah, and Egingwah spring to the fore in any discussions of the North Pole, for ignoring the help seems to be a solid tradition in exploration. That's why you likely don't know either about Denise Martin and Matty McNair from Iqaluit in Canada's Northwest Territories. They were hired by four British women in 1997 to achieve another northern first: crossing the polar sea to the North Pole, on skis. Although Martin and McNair guided, led, and organized the team, and even saved the life of one, their names weren't even mentioned when the four Britons stood at the Pole and videotaped speeches for the British media.

55

Q: She was called "the Divine Sarah," and her biographers claim that for sixty years, not a day went by without a mention of her in the media somewhere. Sarah who?

A: Of course, Sarah Bernhardt (1844–1923), actor, novelist, playwright, sculptor, painter, recording star, and *major* personality.

The Challenge

Q: At the very peak of her stage career, in her own native France, Bernhardt regularly played second fiddle – in audience size – to a wildly popular vaudeville star named Joseph Pujol. What talent enabled Pujol to outshine the great Bernhardt?

A: **He farted,** and Parisian audiences, it seems, couldn't get enough of his amazing derrière. Known by the stage name "le Petomane," Pujol was a leading act at the Moulin Rouge from 1892 to 1914. Among his variations on a theme were flatulent imitations of contemporary opera stars, playing an ocarina through a rubber tube connected to . . . well, you figure it out, and blowing out a candle with one of his zephyrs at a distance of up to one foot (0.3 m). For his encore — he once caused a near-riot by refusing to do it — Pujol would have the audience stand at attention while he solemnly farted the first line of "La Marseillaise."

Unlike Bernhardt, who lived a dramatically unique lifestyle, Pujol was quite staid. The Divine Sarah was known to sleep in a coffin lined with letters from her many lovers. Joseph Pujol indulged in no excesses of that nature, the better perhaps to preserve his skills.

It is interesting that whereas many human ejection habits have met with a varied reception over time (take spitting, for example), breaking wind, especially in front of an audience that has not bought tickets for the privilege, consistently generates three reactions: amusement, annoyance, and embarrassment. Edward de Vere knew all about the third. He was earl of Oxford during the reign of Elizabeth I, and a man who prided himself on his charm and social dexterity. Unfortunately, de Vere once farted during the contortions of an extremely low bow to the queen and was so chagrined that he left the court for several years. When he finally mustered the courage to return, the good queen's welcome was no help at all, for she greeted him with "My Lord, I had forgot the fart."

56

Q: Officially or otherwise, all countries of the world now use the Gregorian calendar, instituted by Pope Gregory XIII in 1582. What calendar did the Gregorian replace?

A: Indeed, the Julian calendar.

The Challenge

Q: For the Gregorian system, the designers chose what they believed to be the date of Jesus Christ's birth as the pivotal point, or point from which the years are numbered forward and backward. What is the pivotal point in the Julian system?

A: **The founding of the city of Rome,** which is pegged by the Gregorian system at 753 B.C.

The Julian calendar was officially instituted in 46 B.C. At the time, the existing Roman calendar was a full three months out of whack (partly because the Roman Senate had fiddled with it to reduce the time in office for certain officials!). Julius Caesar repaired things by inserting sixty-seven extra days into 43 B.C. and decreeing that in 46, and every fourth year thereafter, there would be two February 24s! (You can do these things when you run an empire.) However, the Julian year is eleven minutes longer than the solar year, so by the sixteenth century, the calendar was ten and a half days behind the sun. Enter Pope Gregory, whose basic fix was that a century year must be divisible by 400 to be a leap year. (E.g., 2000 is a leap year, but not 1900.)

In 1582, all the Catholic countries of Europe bought in, and jumped straight from October 4 to October 15. England waited until 1751, moving from March 25 to April 4 despite riots protesting the lost time! The Thirteen Colonies followed in February 1752, and while they were at it, switched New Year's Day from March 25 to January 1. George Washington changed his birthday that year from February 11 to February 22 so he wouldn't miss the party, but he wasn't the first to do something like this. Another notable juggler was Pope Eugenius III. During an official tour in 1147, he had the bad luck to arrive at Paris on a Friday, a day of fasting and abstinence from meat. Because a state banquet had been laid on, there was widespread panic in the kitchens, so Eugenius remedied the situation by simply decreeing the day to be Thursday. No point in being pope if you can't outdo Julius Caesar!

57

Q: *Mercury Theater of the Air*, on CBS, had pretty low ratings on Sunday nights in 1938 because it was up against a very popular show on NBC. All that changed on October 30 with a radio drama that caused a panic across the northeastern part of the continent. What was the name of that radio show?

A: Sure, *War of the Worlds*, Orson Welles's adaptation of a short story by author H. G. Wells.

The Challenge

Q: What was the popular show on NBC?

The Chase and Sanborn Hour, starring Edgar Bergen and Charlie McCarthy.

Bergen, a ventriloquist, along with his smart-mouthed dummy, Charlie, and a few side characters like the terminally stupid Mortimer Snerd, practically owned the airwaves on Sunday nights. Although Welles always insisted he did not intend his Martian invasion to cause a panic – and thereby increase ratings – there is an interesting coincidence to consider. The Welles show began at 8 p.m. that night with "the music of Ramon Raquello and his orchestra coming to you from the Hotel Park Plaza in downtown New York." The music was interrupted by a series of news bulletins about mysterious eruptions on Mars and an interview between announcer Carl Phillips and a Professor Pierson about a humming metal cylinder that had fallen from the skies into New Jersey.

Over at NBC, Bergen's show regularly offered a dial-spinning opportunity at 8:12, for at that point it went to a commercial followed by a guest star appearance, usually a singer. On the fateful night, 8:12 was precisely the time when Phillips and Pierson (who were "live") saw creatures begin to crawl out of the cylinder. The rest, as they say, could only happen in America.

Of the ten million listeners (The show must have worked!), about one million were convinced that Martians had landed. Some citizens roamed New Jersey with guns while others hid in churches or in their basements. Police departments were literally under siege. Defecting NBC listeners had obviously not heard "This is purely a fictional play" at the beginning of Welles's show. They may also have missed three repeats of the caveat. And for sure, they had never read H. G. Wells's original story, for in it the Martians are overcome by good old Earth-based bacteria.

58

Q: Scotland, along with one other country, produces almost all the world's single malt whiskey. What is the other country?

A: Yes, Ireland.

The Challenge

Q: Officially, what is the difference between Scotch and Irish single malt?

A: *Officially,* **the label.** There is, in fact, one other important difference: Irish malts go through three distillations, Scotch malts two. But according to a 1909 British Royal Commission, the only thing that matters is that Scotch is made in Scotland and Irish is made in Ireland.

It all came about when distillers figured out how to make *blended* Scotch in the 1830s. (Basically, blends are made by adding neutral grain alcohol to malt. Chivas Regal, for example, is a blend; so are the Johnnie Walkers.) Devotees of single malt did not consider these new kids on the block to be true whiskies, and a group of publicans in England was successfully prosecuted in 1905 for selling them as such. The pub owners appealed, and when the courts couldn't resolve the issue after seven long sittings, the British government appointed a Royal Commission to decide the matter. The commissioners (there were major backroom battles to get onto this board), after intense and lengthy research, ruled that blends are whiskies and that's that. Almost as an afterthought, they tossed in the official Scotch–Irish distinction that must appear on the label.

The brand names that appear on these labels invariably have a lilting Celtic ring — Laphroaig, Balvhenie, Glen Moranchie — in stark contrast to the names that were popularly applied to whiskies on the North American frontier, names like "skull varnish," "snake water," "forty rod" (how far you'd run after one swallow), and the legendary "red eye." These were often semi-poisonous brews containing flavor and "kick" enhancers like red pepper, soap flakes, and tobacco juice (already chewed!). To control the illegal peddling of this kind of stuff to the native peoples in the West, the Canadian government established the Mounties in 1873.

59

Q: Of Barnum and Bailey, the legendary circus owners who first joined forces in 1881, the better-known half is the flamboyant Barnum. What are his initials?

A: Sure, P. T.

The Challenge

Q: What do they stand for?

A: **Phineas Taylor.** Bailey was J. A., for James Anthony.

Barnum had a bigger name in 1881 but the Bailey name was much more established in the entertainment business. Sixty years before, Hackaliah Bailey had turned a talented female elephant, Old Bet, into a big star. She was the second elephant ever seen in North America. The first had arrived in 1796, but apparently was a klutz.

Neither achieved the fame of Jumbo, a gigantic African elephant that Barnum bought from the London Zoo for $10,000 in 1882. Jumbo was billed as the biggest elephant ever seen, and he was. His record size has never been challenged to this day. In fact, our word "jumbo" for outsized items comes from his name, not the other way around. Jumbo became the biggest draw at the "Greatest Show on Earth," and when he was killed by a freight train in St. Thomas, Ontario, in 1885, circus fans thought Barnum was finished. But if anyone knew how to squeeze a lemon, it was old P. T. He ordered the elephant's skin and skeleton preserved, and for the next two years, two Jumbos, his skeleton and his stuffed skin, led the B&B circus parade on separate wagons, followed by his "widow," Alice, and a herd of smaller elephants trained to hold black-edged sheets in their trunks and, on command, wipe their eyes.

African elephants can grow to a weight of seven tons – about the weight of a newborn blue whale – and are larger than Indian elephants. When Anna May, an Indian elephant, played Jumbo in the movie *The Great Barnum*, she needed buckets of makeup, along with ears and tusks, to come up to size.

60

Q: Where does a young girl named Alice meet an amazing array of characters like the Mad Hatter, the Cheshire Cat, the Queen of Hearts, and others?

A: Yes, in Wonderland.

The Challenge

Q: What is the title of the story by Lewis Carroll?

A: Not *Alice in Wonderland,* but *Alice's Adventures in Wonderland.*

Carroll's original title was *Alice's Adventures Underground.* Also, when he first got the idea by telling stories to little Alice Liddell during a boating trip, most people were still calling this math teacher Charles Lutwidge Dodgson.

Alice was banned in China in 1931, exactly fifty years after Walt Whitman's *Leaves of Grass* had been banned in Boston, where, sixty years before that, North America's first known obscenity case was argued over John Cleland's *Fanny Hill.* The Vatican — no surprise here — banned Martin Luther's *Works* in 1521, and then, just for good measure, banned it again in 1930. Canada, Ireland, and the U.S. actually burned copies of Joyce's *Ulysses* in 1922. In Illinois, Hans Christian Andersen's *Wonder Stories* wasn't burned, but the book was stamped "For Adult Readers" to make it "impossible for children to obtain smut."

Alice lost out in China because animals talked like humans, but curiously, the censors there weren't upset by the oddities of the Mad Hatter. Possibly, they suspected he was a victim of mercury poisoning, something with which they had some sympathy and experience. Hatters used mercury to stabilize wool, and over time the fumes would cause erethism, an intense and abnormal irritability often approaching outright madness. Mercury is obtained by heating the mineral cinnabar. In the 1930s in China, cinnabar was used in the manufacture of that country's ever-popular red banners.

Lewis Carroll himself raised more than one eyebrow with his behavior. One eccentricity he followed faithfully whenever he traveled was to wrap every item in his luggage with a separate piece of paper. Except for his hat.

61

Q: At the end of Shakespeare's *Macbeth*, who kills Macbeth?

A: Right, Macduff.

The Challenge

Q: Is that who killed the real Macbeth?

A. Not according to Holinshed's *Chronicle of Scottish History*, Shakespeare's principal source – mine, too (second edition, if you want to be fussy). The real Macbeth was killed in 1057 by Malcolm, who thereby won back the throne Macbeth had taken from his father, Duncan. As everyone learns by the tenth grade, The Bard was not above fiddling with historical facts to suit his dramatic purposes. (Nor, for that matter, was Holinshed.) Malcolm not only had to defeat Macbeth, but in 1058 he also had to take out Macbeth's son, Lulach. Very little is known about Lulach except for the moniker bestowed by his contemporaries: Lulach the Fatuous. Apparently, he was not a candidate for the gifted class.

Macbeth met his end on August 15, which is an auspicious day for comings and goings in history. It's the birthday of modern India (1947), for example, and the Republic of South Korea (1948), and it's also the day, in 1769, that Carlo Bonaparte and Maria Ramolino had a baby boy in Corsica. August 15 is the birthday, in 1860, of Florence Kling, later Florence Kling *DeWolfe*, and then after that, Florence Kling DeWolfe *Harding* when she divorced DeWolfe and married the man who would become the twenty-ninth president of the United States. Florence is remembered for walking into the Oval Office one day without knocking, somewhat to the surprise of the commander-in-chief, who was busily engaged atop a desk – and a secretary. Fortunately, August 15 also offers a moral counterpoint to this event each year, for it's the day the Vatican picked to celebrate the assumption of the Blessed Virgin Mary into heaven.

While you have your notebook out: on August 15, Guy Zinn of the New York Yankees stole home twice in the same game. That was in 1912.

62

Q: When Alexander Graham Bell said, "Mr. Watson, come here. I want you," he was making what many believe to be a world first. The world's first what?

A: Indeed, first telephone call.

The Challenge

Q: Why did Bell want Watson to "come here"?

A: **Bell had just spilled acid in his lap,** making this first call, in effect, a 9-1-1 emergency!

Bell's achievement is really a "stolen by America" legend for fifteen years earlier, in 1861, Johann Philipp Reis had already demonstrated his working telephone to German scientists at a meeting of the Physical Society of Frankfurt. The sound quality was not great, because the diaphragm on the mouthpiece was a stretched sausage skin (which opens an entire arena of speculation about people with odd telephone habits), but Reis's device definitely transmitted sound, which is why so many Europeans don't accept Bell as first. Another forgotten name in telephone history is that of Elisha Gray. In February 1876, just a few hours after Bell filed his notice of intent to patent a telephone, Gray walked in to file his; he was *that* close. Nor was Gray alone: from 1876 to 1893, Bell had to fight off over 600 lawsuits for patent infringement.

Nothing remotely as contentious developed over the electric flowerpot, patented around the same time as the telephone. This device was a slender battery in a tube with a lightbulb at one end, designed to illuminate flowers. It didn't sell, so the inventor, Joseph Lionel Cowan, sold the rights to an employee, Conrad Hubert, who modified the design a bit and then founded the Eveready Flashlight Company. Cowan was not resentful, however, for not long after, he got rich when his design for toy electric trains caught on.

It's interesting to speculate whether Bell's first telephone words were issued calmly, inasmuch as his crotch was in considerable danger, but we'll never know, because the first magnetic-tape recorder didn't appear until 1929.

◁ ▷

63

Q: "Checkered career" is a phrase we often hear, and English clergyman John Newton (1725–1807) certainly had one. He was press-ganged into the navy, became an officer, and then turned deserter. After he was ordained, he wrote words for a hymn in which he confessed that "I once was lost, but now I'm found. Was blind, but now I see." According to Newton, something "saved a wretch like me." What was it?

A: Right, amazing grace.

The Challenge

Q: Why did Newton confess to being "a wretch"?

A: **He'd been the captain of a slave ship.** His wish to make amends is wonderfully reflected in the words he wrote for "Amazing Grace." Credit for the beautiful tune, however, must go to good old "Anon." It's from an old folk piece.

Newton's hymn appeared in 1779, just in time to influence a young career soldier in the British military, John Graves Simcoe. Just how much, we can never know, but in 1792, when Simcoe arrived in Upper Canada (now Ontario) as lieutenant-governor, one of the first things he did — besides starting the present-day city of Toronto — was to declare slavery illegal. At the time, England was still forty years away from doing this, and in the newly formed U.S.A., George and Martha Washington between them owned over 300 slaves.

It was many, many years later that Emperor Menelik II (he of the electric-chair throne; see page 42) abolished slavery in Abyssinia (now Ethiopia). Like John Newton, Menelik was very much influenced by the Bible, although he used this holy book somewhat differently than most. To treat his illnesses, especially his frequent seizures, he would eat pages from various books of the Old Testament. It is not known whether Menelik ate copies of hymns, but if he did, "Amazing Grace" would have been a clear choice over *Hora Novissima Tempora*, a twelfth-century effort by Abbot Bernard of Cluny. At 2,966 lines it is the longest known hymn. "Amazing Grace" is a mere snack by comparison: only sixteen lines (twenty if you repeat the first verse at the end; most renditions do).

64

Q: Picture James Cagney dancing and singing this line in a 1942 movie: "I'm a Yankee doodle dandy, born on the fourth of July." Who was Cagney portraying?

A: Sure, George M. Cohan.

The Challenge

Q: When was Cohan born?

A: On the *third* of July, in **1878,** to an Irish family originally named Keohane.

In his relatively brief sixty-six years on Earth, Cohan wrote more than 500 songs (e.g., "Give My Regards to Broadway," "Over There," "Mary's a Grand Old Name") and 41 musicals and plays (e.g., *The Song and Dance Man, The Little Millionaire*), and produced 130 others. Such prodigious accomplishment was helped by the fact that, like many stars who began in the vaudeville era, he started in early childhood.

Cohan himself picked Cagney for the starring role in the movie *Yankee Doodle Dandy*, despite initial objections at Warner Bros. because of Cagney's image as a "tough-guy." In fact, Cagney had been a Broadway hoofer before Hollywood and took to the role well enough to win an Academy Award for best actor (over notables like Gary Cooper, Ronald Colman, and Walter Pidgeon). But it didn't come easily. Cagney trained for four months to perfect the stiff-legged Cohan style and the "hitch" that future impressionists would adopt wholesale, and in the process sprained his ankle twice. Such devotion to the craft was typical for Cagney. He was known for his ability to cry on cue, and during the filming of *Yankee Doodle Dandy*, bawled so convincingly in the death-of-his-father scene that director Michael Curtiz burst into uncontrollable sobs and ruined the take.

As you probably know, James Cagney was not born on the fourth of July. Nor was England's George III. Of note, however, is the entry for July 4, 1776, in George's personal diary: "Nothing of importance happened today."

Q: In 1491, King James IV of Scotland passed a law ordering young men to stop "beating up pastures with a stick [playing] that silly game." What "silly game" was he talking about?

A: Sure, golf.

The Challenge

Q: When did the Olympics put a stop to golf?

A: During the 1908 Games. Golf was a medal event in 1900 and 1904 but was dropped in 1908 when a boycott left only one entrant, a Canadian, George Lyon, and he declined to accept the gold by default. Lyon already had a golfing gold, anyway. At the 1904 Olympics in St. Louis, he shocked U.S. fans by defeating their champion (who was exactly half George's age).

George Seymour Lyon was a character of the first order. He didn't start playing golf until he was thirty-eight (the gold medal came at forty-six), although he was a baseball, cricket, and tennis player and held a Canadian record in pole-vaulting! American newspapers laughed at Lyon's odd golf swing (he used the club like a cricket bat), until they saw his drives average close to 300 yards — in the days of wooden shafts. Lyon was an entertainer, too. He would sing to the crowd as it followed him down the green, and tell jokes, or do handstands. At the medal ceremony, he walked to the podium on his hands and received what several reporters described as the loudest applause at the 1904 Games!

The demise of golf as a medal event wasn't really the fault of the sport. Racquetball also died that year, as did lacrosse and polo. As usual, the culprit was politics. The 1900 Games in Paris had been badly run; in St. Louis four years later, the organization had been even worse. So in 1908, in London (a second choice; Italy was supposed to host but couldn't get its act together), the British took such complete and officious charge that most of the energy that year was taken up with international squabbling.

66

Q: Mong Kut became king of Siam in 1851. While his name may not spring readily to the lips, that's not usually the case for the name of a young lady he employed to look after his children. Who was that young lady?

A: Yes, Anna.

The Challenge

Q: Anna who?

A: Leonowens. She never rose above the status of a minor servant in the royal court, and never got a raise because the king felt her work was unsatisfactory. In her defense, being governess in Mong Kut's court must have involved little more than crowd control. Mong was a Buddhist priest in his youth and had taken a vow of celibacy, so when he came to the throne he had only twelve children. But by 1867, he'd managed to father another eighty-two. (Hard to know when he had time to evaluate his staff!)

In the movies, Anna brings Western enlightenment to Siam, but the real Anna was far less influential. Had she been the power we are led to believe, it's possible she might have introduced a form of birth control — albeit inadvertently — by means of a Victorian fashion: corsets. In the 1830s, newly invented metal eyelets made extreme "tightlacing" possible, and fashion leaders decreed that the wasp waist was in. The result, for middle- and upper-class ladies in Europe and North America, was contraception by corset. Waistlines were yanked in to an average of 60 percent of normal, causing significant internal organ changes. Women complained to their diaries about unending constipation, backaches, dizziness, and severe pain during "the family duty." Some medical historians speculate that the corset disrupted the ovulation cycle and thereby lowered the birthrate. Whether or not that theory explains it, the fact is that fertility rates for middle-class women in the West were down by 11 percent by the 1850s and by 26 percent in 1890.

Siam became the Kingdom of Thailand in 1949, the same year that cortisone was first used to treat arthritis.

67

Q: Our word "alphabet" comes from *alpha* and *beta*, the first two letters of the Greek alphabet. The alphabet used in Russia also gets its name from Greece, specifically from a saint who came from Thessaloniki. What is that alphabet called?

A: Right, the Cyrillic alphabet, after Saint Cyril (c. 827–69), who with his brother, Saint Methodius (c. 825–85), translated the Christian Scriptures for the Slavic peoples.

The Challenge

Q: Our alphabet has twenty-six letters. How many does the Cyrillic alphabet have?

A: Thirty-two.

By the time the Romans finished working on the alphabet handed on to us (they got it from the Greeks, via the Etruscans, and the Greeks got theirs from the Phoenicians), there were twenty-three letters in use. After the Romans faded, scribes in England and France gradually added the "u" and the "w", bringing the number up to twenty-five. In the fifteenth century, "j" became the Johnny-come-lately. It developed to replace "i" whenever it had a *dz* sound at the beginning of words. (The military still avoids "i" and "j" because they are so easily confused.)

In spelling class, it used to be a safe bet that the letter "u" would unfailingly follow "q" (as in "quagga" and "quetzal"), but dictionaries have become more international now and recognize that some languages, such as Arabic, don't always do this. Nor does Inuktitut, a language spoken by aboriginal peoples of the Canadian Arctic. It's a language that until this century did not even have an alphabet. The use or non-use of the "u" can be extremely important to the Inuit. For example, in 1987, the Baffin Island community of Frobisher Bay became the first Arctic town without a "u" after the "q" when it reverted to its former name, Iqaluit, which means "the place where the fish are." With the "u"s the word (i.e., "iqualuit") means "unclean buttocks," which is why Canadians, by and large, have learned to be very careful when addressing letters to their friends there.

"Quagga," by the way, is a Hottentot word for a zebra-like animal, which although it is extinct, has nevertheless retained its "u." The quetzal is a bird with a "u" and very long tail feathers. This tail, like the "u", does not come off during molting.

Q: Car-making brothers Fred and August had no trouble picking a name for the wickedly fast Duesenbergs they started building in 1919; they simply used the family name, Duesenberg. Brothers Gaston and Louis went the same route in naming the Chevrolet. And so did brothers Horace and John, whose surname is still an important brand name in the Chrysler organization. That name?

A: Yes, Dodge.

The Challenge

Q: What name did car-manufacturing brothers Freelan and Francis choose?

A: **The Stanley (Steamer).** Their first steamer rolled out of the shop in 1897.

Not a new discovery, the steamer — that happened in France, back in 1769 — but the Stanley brothers' buggy was a thing to be admired. No transmission, no spark plugs, clutch, or gearshift, no pollution, and only fifteen moving parts. Almost nothing went wrong with the cars, and if anything did, the brothers would take the offender back to the factory and fix it for free. By 1906, for anyone nuts enough to try, Stanleys could do 128 mph (206 km/h) on the straightaway! The principal inconveniences were the time it took to get up steam, the need to add water frequently, and a perception — not really accurate, but exploited by the internal combustion supporters in Detroit — that steamers would blow up. All these problems had been overcome when the last Stanley was made in 1925, but by then, steam had lost out to gasoline. The slide had begun when Charles Kettering perfected the electric starter in 1911, and became inevitable when Henry Ford's assembly line took the Model T to unprecedented low prices. The Stanleys didn't really care a whole lot anyway. Even in their "down" years, they wouldn't sell a steamer to someone unless they felt like it!

The Stanley appeared four years *after* North America's first gasoline-powered car. That one was built, not in Detroit, but in Springfield, Massachusetts, by yet another set of brothers, Charles and Frank Duryea. Like the Wright brothers, the Duryeas were bicycle mechanics. The world's first electric car was an English creation in 1874. However, its future was pretty much forecast by the fact that cloth-covered tennis balls, introduced for the first time that same year, caused a much bigger stir in London.

69

Q: What novelist said that everybody talks about the weather but no one does anything about it?

A: Sure, Mark Twain.

The Challenge

Q: What novelist did try to do something about it?

A. **Charles Dickens.** In August 1848, he began to publish weather reports in his newspaper, the *Daily News*. Conditions at a variety of weather stations in England were analyzed, collated, and then printed the following day. It wasn't true weather news as we know it today because the reader was told only what *was*, not what *was to be*, and thus had to decide for him- or herself whether to take along an umbrella. Real prediction service didn't come until *The Times* started doing it in 1861, using essentially the same sources that Dickens's paper had. *The Times* called the practice "forecasting" on the premise that "prognostication" or "prophecy" had too much of a psychic flavor.

Although European readers were intrigued by the new service, they continued to rely on observations that had proven useful for generations: e.g., when rain is imminent, sheep's wool tends to lose its curl and frogs croak. These phenomena are in response to the drop in atmospheric pressure, although most *Times* readers were not aware of that (nor were the frogs, and certainly not the sheep!). Also operating by instinct are fiddler crabs, which move inland up to two days before a storm, and ants, which seek higher ground when really bad weather is on the way. However, the track record of ants makes them less than reliable, since they also move en masse for other reasons. A somewhat more impressive record can be claimed by former UCLA geophysics professor G. J. F. MacDonald. In 1968, he predicted that by 1988, satellites would be used to beam weather information to anywhere in the world. (He also said that by 2018, weather will be manageable in such a way that drought and storms can become weapons of aggression.)

70

Q: Between 1914 and 1916, Gustav Holst composed what is likely his best-known piece of music. What is its title?

A: Right, *The Planets*.

The Challenge

Q: Of the movements named after various planets, "Jupiter" is the most often heard. "Saturn" is popular, too; so are "Mars" and "Neptune." On the other hand, the "Uranus" movement is rarely heard; ditto for "Mercury." And "Pluto" is never heard at all. Why not?

A: There is no such movement. When Holst composed *The Planets*, Pluto wasn't known. When an amateur astronomer picked it out in 1930, Holst was only fifty-six, but he was never healthy and was not disposed to fill in the blank.

Among other ailments, Holst suffered so badly from neuritis in his right arm that to write music, he often had to have a pen nib tied to his finger and then would use his upper body to drag it across the paper. The neuritis also ended any hope of his becoming a concert pianist, but as a would-be composer he had to be proficient with some instrument, so he took up the trombone by default. A bit of serendipity, for the choice enabled him to get control of his asthma.

One musician who did succeed as a concert pianist against overwhelming odds was Clara Wieck Schumann (1819–96). The hurdles she faced were a) being a woman – a Viennese critic said that Clara could be called the greatest living pianist, "were the range of her physical strength not limited by her sex" – and b) marrying Robert Schumann in 1840. Robert was committed to an asylum twelve years later but Clara still bore eight babies, an on-task rate that must surely have limited her time to practice! She continued to compose, however, something she'd done since about age fifteen. Not quite in Mozart's category for being precocious – he'd finished his fourteenth symphony by that age – but on a par with Fanny Mendelssohn, sister of Felix, who at thirteen could play all of Bach's *Well-Tempered Clavier* from memory. Chopin was only seven when he wrote the Polonaise in G Minor.

When he discovered Pluto, Clyde Tombaugh was twenty-four.

Q: Margaret Gorman was the first person to win this title in a contest that was then, and is now, open only to women. She won the distinction in Atlantic City, New Jersey, where the contest is traditionally held. What is the title?

A: Right, Miss America.

The Challenge

Q: The first Miss America pageant was held in 1921, but the first beauty pageant ever in modern times was held in Europe in 1888. In what country?

A. **No, not France, but close: Belgium.** The winner was an eighteen-year-old Creole girl from Guadeloupe named Bertha Soucaret. Very little is known about her, for the finalists were hidden from everyone but the judges. That was not at all the case for Margaret Gorman and the rest in Atlantic City, where they paraded publicly in every event. Gorman, who came into the contest as Miss Washington DC, was and still is a five-way record holder: first to win; first to appear in a bathing suit (along with the other competitors); youngest (she was only fifteen and still in high school); shortest (5 feet 1 inch); and thinnest (her measurements were 30-25-32).

The Miss America pageant was the inspiration of Herb Test, a reporter with the *Atlantic City Press*, who worked very hard to make the contest a fair one. Whether or not fairness prevailed in the world's first official dog show, however, is still being debated. It was held in 1859, in Newcastle upon Tyne, and was open only to setters and pointers. There were thirty entries in each class. The pointer winner was a liver-and-white male owned by Mr. R. Brailsford, while the setter title went to a red male owned by Mr. J. Jobling. Coincidentally, Mr. Jobling was judge of the pointers, while Mr. Brailsford evaluated the setters.

Competitors in the Miss America contest are allowed to wear contact lenses, but only if they are prescribed, and only if they are clear (i.e., uncolored). In dog shows, discretion in the matter of contact lenses is left to individual judges. The first dog in Spain to be fitted with contacts (in 1982, in Bilbao) ran under a car and died the very next day. His name was Stan.

72

Q: Tests of the left #1: one of the first adjustments a North American has to make in England is driving on the left. Are there other countries that do this?

A: Yes indeed. There are over fifty countries (e.g., Kiribati, Tuvalu, the Cook Islands) besides England where the right way to go is left.

The Challenge

Q: Tests of the left #2: now, don't move your hands, and don't look! On your shirts, which side has the buttons, and which side the buttonholes?

A: Buttons are on the left for women and on the right for men. For the right-handers – the majority – it's easier to push buttons on the right through holes on the left. How women's clothing came to be the opposite has more to do with social history than with sinister plotting by gender warriors. When buttons came into popular use in the thirteenth century, replacing pins, belts, and hooks, they were used pretty exclusively by the wealthy. Men generally dressed themselves, but women were usually assisted by servants – right-handed servants, mostly – who faced their mistresses and buttoned away. Not many servants are used today, but the tradition of button placement hangs on.

No one knows if Jack the Ripper had trouble buttoning up, but Scotland Yard is 99 percent certain he was left-handed. So was Queen Victoria. Neil Armstrong stepped onto the moon left foot first. Captain Ahab would likely not have, if given the chance, for it was his left leg that was missing, as was Captain Hook's left hand and part of Vincent van Gogh's left ear. Despite the fact that left-handers often have trouble using regular scissors and playing saxophones, and although no leftie has ever won the world championship of horseshoe pitching, the news is not all bad. Lefties find it easier to write Hebrew and unscrew jar tops.

Polar bears always use the left paw in attack and defense. Haakon IV of Norway once gave a polar bear to England's Henry III. He gave one to Frederick II of Austria, too. Both Henry and Frederick were right-handed. We're not sure about Haakon.

73

Q: What did Salome request of King Herod, around the year A.D. 30?

A: Yes, the head of John the Baptist on a platter.

The Challenge

Q: What did Katie Casey request of Jack Norworth in 1908?

A: **"Take me out to the ball game!"** Katie asked, "[and] buy me some peanuts and Cracker Jack." The song is one of the best-known sports ditties in English, and can be sung with reasonable accuracy even by people who have never seen a professional baseball game. That could be because the two men responsible for the song never saw a professional game either until their song became popular. Vaudevillian Jack Norworth got on an EL train one day in Manhattan and saw a poster advertising a game. Before he reached his stop he had finished the lyrics. Fellow entertainer Albert von Tilzer then wrote the music.

What we know of Salome comes mostly from Jewish historian Joseph ben Matthias (A.D. 37–?). Although she danced in Matthew 14:6–11 and in Mark 6:22, neither her name nor her "Seven Veils" dance is mentioned in the Bible. This information comes from Joseph. However, it's entirely possible that he was as much of an expert on Salome as Norworth and von Tilzer were on baseball. After leading a Galilean force against the Romans in a first-century Jewish revolt, Joseph switched sides, became Flavius Josephus, and went to live in Rome – a move that may well have affected his point of view.

Katie Casey appears in the first verse of Norworth's song. There's still debate over whether she was real. Casey Jones was real – and a hero. He was John Luther Jones, who died at the throttle of his runaway express in 1900, trying to minimize the potential loss of life. "Casey at the Bat," however, is fictional. In 1888, Ernest Lawrence Thayer got $5 from the *San Francisco Examiner* for the poem. Since he was already a millionaire, it's likely he blew the five bucks on a good time.

74

Q: A character in an old movie takes out a pocket watch and says, "The Limited is due tonight at 11:37." What is a "Limited"?

A: Right, a train (and sometimes, but rarely, a bus).

The Challenge

Q: What is limited on a "Limited"?

A: The number of stops. Usually, a "Limited" was a long-distance service with extended first-class accommodations so wealthier passengers would not have to go elbow to elbow with the great unwashed, an issue in rail travel from its very beginning. Seminal proof that the latter tend to push their way onto trains unbidden was established on the world's very first train trip. In Wales, in 1804, a foundryman bet an engineer (who should have known better) that a locomotive built by Richard Trevethick could pull five carloads of iron over 9.75 miles (15.7 km) of track. The locomotive was little more than a steam engine on a wagon chassis but it completed the run without a stop. By the end of the line, seventy people had climbed on for the ride.

Surely, it was this kind of behavior that caused the duke of Wellington to object to the idea of passenger trains, for as the Iron Duke (he was Britain's prime minister at the time) was heard to observe, such a service would "cause the lower classes to move about." One of the duke's cabinet colleagues, William Huskisson, must have taken that position very much to heart. In 1830, at the grand opening of the Liverpool and Manchester Railway, he took advantage of his upper-class immunity in the matter of rules and regulations and imprudently crossed the tracks to have a word with Wellington. Huskisson was run over by a locomotive, thereby becoming the first person ever to be killed in a railway accident.

This would never have happened in Iceland, because there are no railways there. No snakes, either. Or upper classes.

75

Q: In 1961, John F. Kennedy electrified the whole of Germany when he proclaimed from the podium, "*Ich bin ein . . . !*" "*Ich bin ein*" what?

A: Yes, "*Berliner.*"

The Challenge

Q: What is the translation?

A: To Berliners, his audience, it was slang for "I'm a doughnut." But the huge crowd, after a few seconds of shock, knew instinctively what Kennedy really meant. At the time, the cold war made Germany, especially the divided city of East and West Berlin, one of the hottest spots in Europe, and Kennedy's declaration of support was warmly welcomed even if his advisers had missed the slang. Twenty years earlier, a comment aimed at Germany almost got Mohandas (Mahatma) Gandhi in trouble, but he too was forgiven. In the June 22, 1941, issue of the Indian daily *Harijan*, Gandhi praised "a genius, a brave man, a matchless organizer and much more." He was writing about Adolf Hitler!

Not that either Gandhi or Kennedy lead the way in the regrettable public statement category. In the 1930s, influential writer H. G. Wells, after he met Josef Stalin, said he'd "never met a man more candid, fair and honest . . . no one is afraid of him and everybody trusts him." But then, writers are perhaps more given than most to ill-thought-out pronouncements. The poet Byron once declared that Shakespeare was overrated and ultimately would prove to be a bust. He also predicted that as soon as people started thinking about good literature a little more deeply, Chaucer's status would be eclipsed by that of Thomas Erceldourne.

Conceivably, this tendency to pass on authoritative wisdom undermines the speaker most when he steps outside his own field. John Ruskin, author of *The Stones of Venice*, a massive tome that is still seen as a landmark analysis of architectural philosophy and design, offered this insight on Beethoven in 1885: "[His musical works] sound like the upsetting of a bag of nails with here and there an also dropped hammer."

76

Q: What units are used to describe the height of a horse?

A: Sure, hands.

The Challenge

Q: How big is a "hand"?

A: Four inches (10 cm). Racehorses are generally about 15 to 16 hands. The tallest horse ever documented is Mammoth, a shire horse foaled in 1846, who grew to 21.5 hands. His weight at maturity (3,360 lb., or 1,570 kg) would have put him in the full-size class at Hertz!

Hopalong Cassidy's horse was of only average height but was named Topper. (His first name, by the way — Hoppy's, not the horse's — was William.) In the TV series *Bonanza*, Hoss Cartwright rode Chub, while on *The Rocky and Bullwinkle Show*, the vacuous Dudley Do-Right called his steed Horse. Over on *Gunsmoke*, Festus Haggin's mule was Ruth, while Matt Dillon's horse was Buck. In the early days of that series, Burt Reynolds was Dodge's blacksmith, but he either walked or took the train. (Worth noting is that Ruth, as a mule, was the offspring of a male donkey and a mare horse. With parents the other way round, Ruth would have been a hinny.) In the first *Godfather* movie, the decapitated horse was Khartoum. Czar Nicholas II called his favorite racehorse Krepysh. The Bolsheviks put Krepysh before a firing squad in 1919.

Horses are unaffected by tear gas, have no collarbone, and can turn their ears independently. So can llamas, but they have bad breath. Both horses and llamas have shorter tongues than okapis, which can wash their own ears if they want to. The first European to see an okapi (in 1901) was Sir Harry Johnston. The sighting was actually a mild disappointment because his expedition was looking for unicorns!

In the Third Reich, German farmers were forbidden to name their horses Adolf. The Führer's name was also forbidden for mountains, roses, church bells, and tarts.

77

Q: In November 1895, German physicist Wilhelm Roentgen discovered mysterious rays that would pass through flesh. What did he call these strange rays?

A: Yes, X-rays.

The Challenge

Q: What did the "X" stand for?

A: **Nothing,** because Roentgen wasn't sure what he had discovered.

The "X" in the name may have contributed to the wide distrust of X-rays at first. Roentgen's wife, for one, wouldn't go near his machine after she saw the bones in her hand. London's *Pall Mall Gazette* called it a "revolting machine" (despite Roentgen's being awarded the first-ever Nobel Prize for physics), and the New Jersey state government introduced a bill to forbid X-rays in opera glasses. By 1900, an English clothing manufacturer was advertising X-ray-proof clothing for "naturally modest ladies."

"X" has a history as a symbol for a kiss, a practice from the days when illiterate people signed documents with an "X" and then kissed it to show sincerity. Max Kiss, on the other hand, never signed his name "Max X," nor kissed his signature, but he's responsible for a chapter in the history of this letter. As a pharmacist, Kiss was well aware of the prevailing attitude toward ghastly cathartics like castor oil. He was also aware that some of his wine-merchant clients put phenolphthalein into their vats (to check acidity), an additive that gave consumers a case of the trots the next morning. Kiss tried to achieve the same next-morning result (at walking speed) by mixing phenolphthalein with chocolate. The result was positive, pleasant, and, if the consumer didn't treat the product as a candy bar, controllable. Kiss went commercial with it, calling the new product "Bo-Bo." Cute, but it didn't sell. Enter "X." Max first thought "X-Lax" was right, but soon switched to "Ex[cellent]-Lax," the name we're so familiar with today. Nothing to do with kissing, really, but then, when you need the stuff, kissing is probably the last thing on your mind.

78

Q: What precious stone is found in the rock called kimberlite?

A: Indeed, diamonds.

The Challenge

Q: Where do most of the world's diamonds come from?

A: **No, not South Africa, but Australia** (also the leading producer of bauxite). To some extent, Australia's distinction depends on the board at General Electric. In 1955, GE developed a process for making diamonds and today is the largest *manufacturer* of industrial-quality diamonds. GE also knows how to make diamonds of gemstone quality but the process costs more than digging for them in kimberlite.

South Africa, however, gave us the largest diamond in the world. The Cullinan (3,106 carats) was dug up — to be precise, a miner tripped over it — near Pretoria in 1905. It was sent to England *by ordinary registered mail* and 105 stones were cut from it. One of the largest of these is the 530-carat Star of Africa, which, when it's not being used at coronations and such, you can see at the Tower of London, for it's part of the British crown jewels. What you can't see at the Tower are what gemologists maintain are two of the most beautiful stones ever cut: the Florentine, a 137-carat double rose the Medicis and Pope Julius II once owned (it was stolen from the Austrian royal family in 1920), and a 280-carat stone called the Mogul (this one disappeared after the siege of Delhi in 1739).

Most stories about stealing jewels suggest the operation is always complex and carefully planned. Perhaps so, but not in the case of Admiral of the Fleet Sir Cloudesley Shovell, who in 1707 struggled to shore on the Isles of Scilly after his ship cracked up on the rocks. He wore a beautiful emerald ring, and an old woman clubbed him to death for it, in keeping with the tradition then prevalent on Scilly that any body washed onto the shore was subject to salvage!

79

Q: By what single name do we know the Spanish painter whose handle begins Pablo Diego José Francisco de Paula Juan Nepomuceno Crispin Crispiano de la Santisma Trinidad Ruiz' y . . . ?

A: Right, Picasso.

The Challenge

Q: By what single name do we know the French playwright whose proper handle is Jean-Baptiste Poquelin?

A: **Molière** (1622–73). Not an unusual practice, the single name, particularly in France. François-Marie Arouet was just Voltaire, for example, and Marie-Henri Beyle was Stendhal. Until the twentieth century, and the arrival of cultural icons like Madonna, Twiggy, and Meatloaf, single names did not work well outside France. Charles Dickens tried Boz but he is definitely better known as Dickens. Saki is perhaps the only writer who comes close, but he is equally well known as H. H. (for Hector Hugh) Munro.

Molière wrote under the patronage of Louis XIV and enjoyed the lifelong friendship of Cyrano de Bergerac (the *real* Cyrano), but good connections didn't help his marriage. His union with vivacious Armande Bejart, for whom he wrote some of his best female roles, was by all accounts an unmitigated disaster – an ironic outcome for a playwright whose work often touched on the vicissitudes of matrimony. But then, if art reflects life, Molière was a true mirror. In 1673, while performing the role of the invalid in *The Imaginary Invalid*, he collapsed on stage, and although he finished the performance, he died later that night. Still, French playwrights have a bit of an edge when it comes to DDS (Dramatic Dying Syndrome). Gérard de Nerval, who never used the one-name shtick (but distinguished himself by strolling the streets of Paris with a lobster on a blue ribbon), hanged himself from a lamppost in 1855, using an apron string that he insisted had once been a garter worn by the Queen of Sheba.

De Nerval's output was slim. Unlike that of Picasso, who is credited with 13,000 paintings and designs, 100,000 prints and engravings, and 34,000 book illustrations. Maybe a single name is all he had time for.

80

Q: Given the nursery rhyme description of Mary's little lamb, it is difficult to argue against a diagnosis of obsessive behavior, for the little beast was sure to go everywhere that Mary went. Even to school one day! In fact the only normal element in Mary's lamb, at least on the surface, was its white fleece. How white was it?

A: Right. White as snow.

The Challenge

Q: That covers the basics of the first verse. Now recite the second verse.

He followed her to school one day –
That was against the rule.
It made the children laugh and play
To see a lamb at school.

The author of "Mary Had a Little Lamb" (1830) was Sarah Josepha Hale, editor of the tremendously influential nineteenth-century magazine *Godey's Lady's Book*. Hale was an ardent feminist whose many achievements include participation in the founding of Vassar College (originally Vassar Female College until she got "female" dropped as too vulgar a synonym for "woman"). Curiously, Hale is often vilified by modern-day feminists because she was adamant in her belief that educated women should stay in the home.

A somewhat curious stance, for she had no truck with such notions as equality of the sexes, offering as proof the point that throughout the seven days described in Genesis, God had worked in ascending order, from mere matter, through man, to the ultimate: Eve. That Hale could casually ignore Eve's subsequent shortcomings is entirely believable if you take the time (not to mention the effort!) to read her magnum opus: *Woman's Record; or, Sketches of All Distinguished Women from the Creation to A.D. 1854.* One of the distinguished choices, for example, was Catherine the Great, whose reputation for having used the Russian Imperial Guard as a stud stable was widely acknowledged in the nineteenth century. Hale, however, describes Catherine as merely given to "irregularities."

No such license was taken in the case of Mary's lamb. The nursery rhyme was inspired by a real incident and Hale maintained faithful gender accuracy in her account. An easy step, as several of her contemporaries noted, for only a male lamb would be so simple-minded.

Q: Where was LZ *Hindenburg* landing when she caught fire on May 6, 1937?

A: Correct, Lakehurst, New Jersey.

The Challenge

Q: Where had she taken off?

A: **Frankfurt, Germany.**

For publicity purposes, the *Hindenburg* overflew New York City, but Lakehurst Naval Air Station was one of the few places in the East big enough for her to put down. She was only 78 feet (23.7 meters) shorter than the *Titanic*, and when she came in that May evening, there were 92 navy and 139 civilian personnel waiting on the ground to moor her!

By 1937, only Germany was flying dirigibles commercially, and doing so with an impressive safety record. The year before, LZ *Hindenburg* had made the Frankfurt–Lakehurst trip ten times and flown to Rio seven times. Her predecessor, the *Graf Zeppelin*, whose career included a round-the-world trip in 1929, had flown pretty much incident-free. On that fateful day at Lakehurst, 62 out of the 97 on board survived the fire, but those who died did so to a live radio broadcast, a coincidence that, probably more than any other reason, brought airship travel to a stop. Four years earlier, when the American dirigible USS *Akron* crashed, only three out of 72 made it out alive. Yet only aviation buffs and military historians have ever heard of this airship and its fate.

Without media attention, the *Sultana* disaster, too, is buried in obscurity. When this criminally overloaded river steamer blew up on the Mississippi on April 27, 1865, she took down almost the same number of bodies as the *Titanic*, most of them Union soldiers going home.

Another unknown: in 1928, the year following Charles Lindbergh's famed solo flight across the Atlantic, 14 pilots died trying to duplicate it. Nineteen twenty-eight is also the year Amelia Earhart became the first woman to cross the Atlantic by air. As a passenger, though. During the flight, the two male pilots wouldn't let her touch the controls.

82

Q: Like Wyatt Earp, Sheriff Masterson (1853–1921) was somewhat of a dandy. Also like Earp, he managed a career as both a lawman and a gambler. Although he was born William Barclay Masterson, most of us know him by what nickname?

A: Sure, "*Bat*" Masterson.

The Challenge

Q: How did he get the name "Bat"?

A: From the cane he carried. Masterson had such a reputation for the speed of his draw (he was never defeated in competitions) that he was able to intimidate more lawbreakers with his gold-headed cane than with his favored pair of nickel-plated Colt Peacemakers.

According to believable contemporaries, Billy the Kid was lightning fast, too (with a Colt .41), as was Butch Cassidy, who carried a Colt .45. Wyatt Earp packed a "Buntline Special," a .45-caliber Colt custom-made for him by the dime novelist Ned Buntline. Because it had a 12-inch barrel, Earp didn't need a cane for "buffaloing" (his term for cracking opponents on the head). However, there is evidence that the wannabes willing to take on gunmen like Earp were not too bright – in either their pre- or post-"buffaloed" state. Among the more impressive examples is Joseph T. Grant, who challenged Billy the Kid on January 24, 1880, in Hargrove's saloon at Fort Sumner, NM. Billy asked to examine Grant's gun first, and surreptitiously adjusted the cylinder so that the hammer would strike an empty chamber on the next shot. (Billy won that one.)

Bat Masterson's cane, I should point out, was not just a cosmetic, but rather, a prosthetic aid. In 1876, both Bat and army sergeant Melvin King were courting one Molly Brennan in Sweetwater, Texas. During an altercation, King accidentally shot and killed Molly. The bullet went through her and lodged in Bat's pelvic bone. He limped for the rest of his life.

Although Bat is alleged to have put down over thirty men in gunfights, only two killings are authenticated. One of them was Melvin King.

83

Q: What famous duo gave us *The Pirates of Penzance, HMS Pinafore, Patience,* and many other similar delights?

A: Yes, Gilbert and Sullivan: William S. Gilbert and Arthur S. Sullivan.

The Challenge

Q: What do the "S"s stand for, respectively?

A: **Schwenk (Gilbert) and Seymour (Sullivan).** G&S fans know that the pair's biggest hit, in terms of number of consecutive performances, is *The Mikado*, with 672 performances from opening to close, beginning in 1885. But they're often surprised to learn that *Pinafore* (1878) is nudged out for number two spot by *Patience*. In 1881, *Patience* opened the Savoy Theatre, the first such emporium in the world to use electric lighting.

Electricity owns another paragraph in the G&S story. Thomas Edison once wired a lightbulb into Sullivan's baton so he could conduct in the dark. Since Sullivan was the proud composer of the hymn "Onward, Christian Soldiers," it is interesting to speculate on how he must have reacted when he learned that Edison lit up the busts of New York showgirls in the same way.

Arthur became Sir Arthur in 1883. Gilbert had to wait another twenty-four years for his knighthood, quite possibly because his librettos often left the clear impression that the British upper classes drew heavily from the shallow end of the gene pool. If this was truly Gilbert's opinion, it would certainly have met with the approval of Jewish philanthropist Sir Moses Montefiore. At a dinner one night in London, not far from a performance of *Pinafore*, Montefiore was sitting opposite a member of Gilbert's favorite class who also happened to be a vicious anti-Semite. This worthy, upon being introduced to Sir Moses, opened conversation with the comment that he had just returned from Japan, an unusual country with no pigs and no Jews. To which Montefiore replied, "In that case, you and I should go there so it will have a sample of each."

84

Q: Where are you most likely to see the capital letters "C," "N," and "N" together?

A: Sure, on your TV screen.

The Challenge

Q: Where are you most likely to see the capital letters "Y," "K," and "K" together?

A: **At the end of your zipper.** It's the logo for a Japanese company that now makes most of the world's zippers.

Prevailing wisdom credits Whitcomb Judson with inventing the zipper in 1893, although *Scientific American* says the first patent went to Elias Howe — the sewing-machine man — in 1851. Either way, Howe got nothing out of it, and as for Judson's device (he called it a "Clasp Locker and Unlocker for Shoes"), the public was decidedly underwhelmed. Even when Gideon Sundback, in 1913, patented a model that worked much better — in fact, the one we use today — the market continued to snore.

During World War I, the U.S. armed forces took a real interest in Sundback's "Slide Fastener," and it became widely used on uniforms and equipment. Yet the civilian market was slow to pick up, partly because of the learning curve. In 1920, "slide fasteners" had to be marketed with instructions attached! It was in 1923 that the B. F. Goodrich Company opened the floodgates. It introduced hookless rubber galoshes, along with a new word: "zipper." B. F. himself is credited with coining the name.

One of the keys to the Goodrich success was that wearers didn't have to figure out the new zipper. On the galoshes, it was even easier to use than buttons, for a single yank did the job. Despite this simplicity, zippers didn't appear on men's pants, except experimentally, until 1935. Thirteen years after that, Swiss mountaineer George de Mestral invented Velcro, but it too didn't catch on for a long time. There is nothing unusual about this. Teflon was discovered in 1938, but over two decades passed before it appeared on pots and pans in North American stores.

◁ **85** ▷

Q: From the deck of USS *Minden*, during the early morning of September 14, 1814, a lawyer was inspired to write a poem which eventually became his country's official anthem (but not until 1931). Who was this lawyer?

A: Indeed, Francis Scott Key.

The Challenge

Q: What was the title of the poem?

A: **"The Defense of Fort McHenry."** Somewhat more treasured by trivia buffs is the fact that the music for what soon became "The Star-Spangled Banner" was once a rather sophomoric English pub song, "To Anacreon in Heaven," about a Greek poet with a reputation. The complex and not very melodic tune makes the U.S. anthem extremely difficult to perform well, and Key's words don't always help. The second verse, for example, is very rarely heard, and no wonder. Try singing the first two lines:

On the shore, dimly seen through the mists of the deep,
Where the foe's haughty host in dread silence reposes.

Still, there is more poetry here than one finds in the anthem of the Republic of Belau. Its second verse, for example, begins, "Let's build our economy's protecting fence."

Canada's national anthem has followed an equally torturous path. "O Canada" was written in 1880 (in French) but didn't become official for a hundred years, one reason the medal ceremony band at the 1948 Winter Olympics had such trouble finding a copy of it. The Games were in St. Moritz, Switzerland, that year, and since Canada was a sure bet in hockey and women's figure skating, the Swiss bandleader knew he would need the music for "O Canada." He turned to the logical source, the Canadian Embassy in Berne. No help; they didn't have a copy. Fortunately, a young secretary was willing to sing it for him over the phone. With only hours to spare because the Canadian hockey team was cleaning up, he transcribed her efforts, wrote an arrangement, rehearsed the band, and then at the medal ceremony proudly played "The Maple Leaf Forever."

86

Q: It's no surprise that the most common family name in the world is Chang (also written Chan, in English). What is the most common surname in North America?

A: Of course, Smith.

The Challenge

Q: What is the second most common surname in North America?

A: **Johnson.** If you thought Jones, and many do, it's not even third. Williams is. Jones comes fourth, followed by Brown, Miller, Davis, Anderson, and Thompson. (In China, Chang is followed by Lee, Cheung, Wong, and Ho.)

It stands to reason that Smiths would occupy some important pages in the annals of trivia. Because there are more than 100,000 John Smiths in the English-speaking world at any one time, many Smith parents attempt to distinguish their offspring via the *first* name. Among the more memorable attempts are Kaboodle, Suryat, Everything, and, in a clear attempt to ensure distinction, Smith. Other Smiths have been very happy with their names, most notably the bearded brothers of cough-drop fame. Andrew is on the right of the box, William on the left. That box design dates from 1872, and although Andrew and William are often called Trade and Mark, the Smith part has remained unsullied.

Another notable entry is Gladys Smith, the real name of Mary Pickford, who became "America's Sweetheart" even though she was a Canadian. Another is Frances Octavia Smith, whom we know better as Dale Evans. A favorite is John Smith, saved from death – twice – by Pocahontas. On the other hand, a more forgettable Smith, probably with good reason, is Emma Smith of Nottinghamshire, England, who, as a stunt in 1968, consented to being buried alive for 101 days.

Back to Chang. Estimates vary, but the data indicate between 9 and 12 percent of the population of China have that name. Using the most conservative numbers, a little math shows that, therefore, the number of people named Chang in China is greater than the entire population of all but about a dozen countries in the rest of the world.

87

Q: This hat is associated exclusively with the West, yet its designer/manufacturer, John Stetson, was exclusively an Easterner. How many gallons does this hat allegedly hold?

A: Right, ten.

The Challenge

Q: How many gallons does it really hold?

A: **About three-quarters.** According to the far more logical metric system, it holds precisely three liters.

In a world where Chinese Checkers comes from Sweden and camel-hair brushes are made from squirrel fur, it follows that creaky and intolerably messy measurement systems continue to be used, with England heading the guilt train and the U.S. accepting the inheritance. Although most of the rest of the world works in tens now, these two countries, particularly, continue with things like the "foot," a unit made up by Henry I in about the year 1120 when he decided that a foot would be one-third the length of his arm. (So it's not hard to figure out where "yard" comes from.)

On the other hand, such arbitrariness is mild when one considers that a pound of feathers (in avoirdupois units) is heavier than a pound of gold (in troy units). The reason is simple, if again illogical. In medieval times, the French city of Troyes was a mecca for merchants throughout Europe. To standardize weights, merchants there adopted the "troy pound," made up of twelve "ounces," from *uncia*, Latin for "one-twelfth." Things might have stayed that way except that merchants of bulkier items like coal and potatoes (and feathers) wanted a larger unit and came up with the avoirdupois pound, which has sixteen ounces. And, possibly to keep simplicity at bay, the avoirdupois ounce was set at 437.5 grains, as opposed to 480 grains for the troy ounce.

When all the above is compounded by the fact that the English horn was developed in Vienna, and that the Canary Islands got their name from wild dogs, it is most comforting to know that Grant is buried in Grant's Tomb. Well, technically, he's *entombed* there.

88

Q: By what nickname did Antoine Domino become known?

A: Sure, "Fats." He was rock 'n' roll singer Fats Domino.

The Challenge

Q: By what nickname did Rodolf Wanderone Jr. become known?

A: **"Minnesota Fats,"** the pool shark brought to fame by yet a third large man, Jackie Gleason, in *The Hustler* (1961).

A fourth fat man, one whose mind tipped the scales of Western thought but whose body, when he died, could not be squeezed through the door of his quarters, has never been the subject of a major movie and was never called "Fats" (although at school, in Paris, his nickname was "Dumb Ox"). Thomas Aquinas (1225–74), saint, philosopher, and hugely obese Dominican friar, is proof of the old "not judging a book by its cover" adage. Although he was slow-moving and slow-witted, Aquinas's *Summa Theologica* almost single-handedly put the Christian church into harmony with the real world.

Six hundred years later and thousands of miles away, yet another "fat" imprint was stamped on our world. In 1889, Missouri businessman Chris Rutt was watching a pair of minstrels perform a cakewalk tune called "Aunt Jemima." Within weeks, the image of a large black woman with a red bandanna above her friendly but caricatured face soon appeared on his pancake boxes, and sales took off. In 1893, Aunt Jemima came to life in the person of Nancy Green at the Chicago World's Fair, where she was so popular that a special police detail was needed to protect her booth! Today's Aunt Jemima looks more like the owner of the house than the cook, but the image was so powerfully entrenched that it took years before its quite blatant insensitivity was modified.

Both Nancy Green and Rodolf Wanderone were quick studies. Not Thomas. A favorite trick of his colleagues — and he fell for it repeatedly — was to entice him to the window to see flying donkeys . . . monastery humor!

89

Q: Elephants, supposedly, are terrified of a particular little rodent. The condition is called myophobia – fear of what?

A: Yes, mice.

The Challenge

Q: Is it true?

A. No. Like most fears, myophobia is real, but the suggestion that elephants have it comes mostly from cartoons. However, like many other large ruminant quadrupeds, elephants are easily spooked by sudden movements, and there is some evidence that they have sciaphobia, fear of shadows, which might explain why groundhogs, and not elephants, do the shtick in February.

Phobias are such an intriguing item in our culture that it's often hard to separate the genuine ones – conditions that actually appear in the literature of psychiatry (e.g., ergasiophobia, fear of work, and eosophobia, fear of dawn) – from the jokes (e.g., friendorphobia, fear of forgetting a password, and arachibyturophobia, fear of peanut butter sticking to the roof of the mouth). One of the more common fears is triskaidekaphobia, a well-known sufferer having been Franklin Delano Roosevelt. He wouldn't sit at a table if it was set for thirteen. Edward Hoffman's linonophobia (fear of string) reportedly was both genuine and serious. Field Marshal Gebhard von Blücher, the Prussian general whose timely arrival on the field at the Battle of Waterloo made a hero out of the duke of Wellington, had a morbid fear that he would give birth to an elephant.

Strangely, although phobia words exist for unusual conditions like the fear of becoming infested with worms (helminthophobia) and the fear of virgins (parthenophobia), no phobia word has yet appeared to describe von Blücher's condition. Nor is there a word to describe the manic fear of kangaroos. Since one-third of all automobile accidents in Canberra, the capital of Australia, are kangaroo related, it would behoove the field of psychiatry to come up with one.

90

Q: What is the popular phrase that explains why people want to climb a mountain?

A: Correct, "Because it's there."

The Challenge

Q: Who made it popular?

A: **George Leigh-Mallory,** when the *New York Times* asked him why, after failing twice to get up Mount Everest, he was trying again. A year later (1924), he and Andrew Irvine were 600 feet (183 meters) from the top when fog moved in and they were never seen again. Many mountaineers believe they made it and that somewhere in the snow at the top is their camera with the film to prove it. Credit for first, however, goes to New Zealand beekeeper Sir Edmund Hillary (his phrase: "Well, we knocked the blighter off!") and Nepalese climber "Tiger" Tenzing Norgay (no quote; Tiger was not given to sound bites). Neither man ever said who was the very first.

When Leigh-Mallory and Irvine went up, Mount Everest was officially listed at 29,002 feet (8840 m) by the 1852 India Survey, in which the engineers had measured from six different points and taken an average that turned out to be exactly 29,000 feet. It seemed too improbable so they added two feet. In the survey, Everest was called "Peak XV." Tibetans call it Chomolungma, "Goddess Mother." However, one must be cautious with that word because, pronounced somewhat differently, it means "Lady Cow"!

By the time Hillary and Norgay went up, survey corrections had raised Everest to 29,028 feet (8848 m). Since their trip, over 700 people have climbed Everest and 150 have died trying. A Nepalese, Ang Rita Sherpa, went up ten times before turning fifty. There are even traffic jams now, because the climbing season is fairly short and expeditions that buy their $70,000 permits rush to get up before the permits expire. This prompts the question: is it worth it just because it's there? Not for the view, anyway, according to Hillary. He called it "monotonous."

91

Q: Yes or no: Michelangelo's original *David* is in Florence.

A: Yes, although the sculpture your tour guide will likely show you — in the Piazza della Signoria — is actually a copy. The original is in the Accademia, not far away, but only an expert can tell the difference.

The Challenge

Q: Yes or no: Michelangelo's *David* is in Vienna.

A: **Yes.** In the Kunsthistorisches Museum in Vienna is a *painting* of David by the "other" Michelangelo, Michelangelo Merisi (c. 1565–1609), better known under his byname, Caravaggio.

Although the temper of the "first" Michelangelo, Michelangelo Buonarrotti (1475–1564), was given high profile by Charlton Heston's clenched-jaw portrayal of him in the movie *The Agony and the Ecstasy*, his bile is pale compared to Caravaggio's. In an era of violence, not to mention haphazard record-keeping, Caravaggio acquired a mind-boggling sheet of assault charges, including, in 1604, throwing a plate of artichokes in a waiter's face. A tepid example at first glance, but part of a chronology of charges for "wounding" that indicated something more serious was inevitable. This came about in 1606, when he got into an argument about the score of a tennis match and killed his opponent. Caravaggio had to get out of Rome after this, but the next three years brought only more of the same: assaults, woundings, and other assorted hot flashes. Yet all the while, he was producing exquisite masterpieces on canvas, sublime in their lighting and in their tone and delicacy. As acknowledged with great restraint by *The Encyclopedia of Art*, Caravaggio's spirit was "given to wrath and riot," and there may have been a foreshadowing of this tendency in the paintings of his early career. A sequence of four paintings, *Boy Peeling Fruit, Boy with a Basket of Fruit, Boy with Fruit*, concludes with *Boy Bitten by a Lizard*.

It's interesting to imagine Caravaggio's response if one of his paintings had ever been treated like Matisse's *Le Bateau*. In 1961, it was on display at New York's Museum of Modern Art for forty-seven days before someone noticed it was upside down.

92

Q: Although she's actually standing in New Jersey, most people describe this statue as being in New York. What statue?

A: Sure, the Statue of Liberty, built (in pieces) in France beginning in the mid-1870s and assembled on her New York Harbor pedestal in 1884–85.

The Challenge

Q: Her official name is not the *Statue of Liberty*. What is her proper title?

A: *Liberty Enlightening the World,* with "enlightening" being a key word. Designer Frédéric-Auguste Bartholdi had struggled against Emperor Napoléon III of France, and made sure Liberty's torch was seen to be giving light, not heat. He was supported in that view by project engineer Gustave Eiffel, who at the time was just beginning to mull over the idea of building a big tower in Paris. (No slouch, Eiffel: some years later he also designed the locks for the Panama Canal.) Ironically, Liberty's light was almost unintentionally extinguished by an American, Gutzon Borglum, the sculptor responsible for Mount Rushmore. In 1916, he rebuilt the torch with panes of glass so it could be illuminated from within, but that had to be changed because rust soon threatened to turn Liberty into another *Venus de Milo.*

Liberty not only enlightens the world, she is one of its relatively few female statues. Except for all the monumental tributes to Queen Victoria spread throughout the former British Empire, women are very much underrepresented in world statuary. In Paris, for example, where there are over a thousand statues, only ten are raised to women, and three of those are to Joan of Arc.

Male figures also dominated in the sculpture of ancient Greece, even though one would think that the female body presents a less challenging task in terms of anatomical correctness. However, it could be that the ancients were not terribly concerned about precision. Until about 480 B.C., for example, the testicles on statues of nude males were sculpted as equals. After this date, advocates of anatomical correctness apparently were successful in getting artists to check before chipping, and subsequent statues present the right one as smaller and higher.

93

Q: What Austrian doctor is called the "father of psycho-analysis"?

A: Yes, Sigmund Freud (1856–1939).

The Challenge

Q: In what branch of medicine was Freud trained?

A: **Neurology.** Although his most cited publication is probably *The Interpretation of Dreams*, Freud's early studies in infantile cerebral palsy and aphasia are classics in the field. It was in his attempts to help patients with psychiatric complaints that he began urging them to recall past thoughts and events, especially dreams.

Freud worried about the impact his ideas might have, especially in the United States (a country he called a "gigantic mistake"). As his fame spread, he confided to a friend that he felt as if he were carrying the plague. Yet this uneasiness didn't stop him from analyzing at will. He once said that the writings and paintings of Leonardo da Vinci, for example, suggest a man whose repressed love for his mother prevented normal heterosexual development. Granted, da Vinci's garbled writings often hint at something strange (sample sentence: "On the 16th of July, Caterina came on the 16th of July 1493."), but oddities are common in the writing of ambidextrous people. In the enigmatic smile of the Mona Lisa, Freud saw da Vinci's "two mothers": his father's wife, who raised him, and the mother who bore him out of wedlock. The two women in *Virgin and Child with St. Anne* apparently confirmed the diagnosis for Freud.

Interestingly, he would have had to examine these paintings face on, quite contrary to the style he established for office visits, i.e., sitting behind the patient, out of sight. That practice has its own justifying literature now, but Freud said the reason he started doing it was because he couldn't stand looking at human faces for eight hours a day!

94

Q: The unit of measurement called the watt is named after James Watt, and the ohm after Georg Ohm. What is named after André-Marie Ampère?

A: Sure, the amp.

The Challenge

Q: What is named after Dieter Volt?

A: **Nothing,** (except, maybe, Dieter Jr.). Dieter Volt drives a bus in Stuttgart. The volt is named after Alessandro Giuseppe Volta (1745–1827), inventor of the wet cell battery. Volta had been devoting most of his investigative skills to analysis of swamp gas when, in 1791, Luigi Galvani discovered the principle of electrical current while dissecting a frog. (Luigi was big on swamps, too.) A few years earlier, Volta had been impressed by Ben Franklin's work, and it was not long before he put two and two (i.e., Ben and Luigi) together.

Another two-plus-two electrical story is that of the lightbulb. Anyone who cares about these things knows that despite the cherished myth, Thomas Edison did not invent the incandescent lightbulb. What he did was improve it, and he was late even with that. Lightbulbs – albeit inefficient ones – had been around for over fifty years before Edison hit upon the idea of using carbon for the filament. That was in 1879, a year later than Joseph Swan, who did it in England in 1878. What then became a suit-countersuit spat eventually turned into a type of shotgun marriage when Swan and Edison co-founded an electric company.

Earlier in the century, Sir Humphry Davy took time off from his work with laughing gas to discover that electricity helps to decompose compounds into elements, and then discovered potassium, sodium, strontium, calcium, and magnesium. He also invented the miner's safety lamp (the Davy lamp) and became the honorary patron saint of proctologists by coming up with barium in 1808. Even earlier than that (1669), alchemist Hennig Brand, although he was not working with electricity, nevertheless shocked himself by discovering phosphorus while analyzing urine. Neither substance is named after him.

95

Q: Tennyson's poem "The Charge of the Heavy Brigade" is relatively unknown, and a quick skim is enough to indicate why. His "The Charge of the Light Brigade," however, is one of the most easily recognized pieces in all of English poetry. It begins

Half a league, half a league, half a league onward.
Into the valley of death rode the . . .

Rode the how many?

A: Correct, the "six hundred." (Actually, there were 673, but try getting that into a line of anapestic tetrameter!)

The Challenge

Q: How far is half a league?

A: **Just under a mile and three quarters (1.726 mi.).** Or, if you'd prefer it in kilometers, it's 2.778.

The North Valley outside Sebastopol, where the seventh earl of Cardigan led the Light Brigade into the Russian guns — at a *trot* — is only one and a quarter statute miles long, a mere third of a league. Which means Tennyson decided that good math makes lousy poetry, for he's got the cavalry covering enough ground to cross the valley almost five times!

The Light Brigade actually did reach the Russian guns that day in 1854, but only 195 cavalrymen made the ride back again. From the rim of the valley, troops on both sides had watched the charge in awe, but even being a mere spectator in the Crimean War was no assurance you would go home some day. The battle-related death rate in that war was 35 per 1,000 combatants. The death rate from disease was 190! (Compare that to the U.S. Civil War a decade later, in which the rates were 20 and 71 per 1,000, respectively.)

Lord Cardigan, one of the 195 survivors, is often portrayed as quite cerebrally challenged, and his behavior as a military commander perhaps justifies this. He purchased his lieutenant-colonelcy in 1830 and prior to the Crimea had developed a reputation for extreme stubbornness and an entirely unforgiving temper. In 1840, he fought a duel with one of his own officers. Yet no one has ever disputed Cardigan's cool during the famous charge. Not only did he trot into the guns, he came all the way back along the North Valley under heavy fire, again at a trot because, as he later explained, it would have been undignified for a commanding officer to retreat at a gallop.

96

Q: What is the most densely populated country in the world?

A: Yes, Bangladesh.

The Challenge

Q: What is the least densely populated country in the world?

A: **Mongolia,** where the population is spread out at a density just below the distribution in both the state of Wyoming and the province of Saskatchewan. Getting lost in these latter two jurisdictions is not all that different from getting lost in Mongolia, because it's hard to find someone to ask directions. What distinguishes them from their far-Eastern counterpart, however, is the existence of useful and accessible maps. Among Mongolians, these aids have never been a very hot item in the gas stations – assuming you can find a gas station.

It could be because of the Siberian experience. For centuries, Mongolians turned to Siberia to practice their raiding skills, and since Siberia's density was not all that different from back home, the Mongolians had to go a long way to find a cluster of population large enough for worthwhile looting and pillaging. Because they often got lost in the process, the raiders developed a clever solution: they rode on mares that had recently foaled, but left the foals behind. When the raiding was finished, they simply turned the mares loose. The mares followed their instincts, the raiders followed the mares, and everyone got home safely.

Homing pigeons would have been another possibility, I suppose, but they don't have foals. Penguins, too, have a well-developed homing instinct, seemingly being able to pick just the right ice floe to take them back across miles of open ocean to their nesting grounds. However, there's no evidence the Mongolians ever tried penguins. Or pigeons. They're not approved for use in Wyoming or Saskatchewan, either.

97

Q: Whose cow is alleged to have started a major fire by kicking over a lantern on the night of October 8, 1871?

A: Sure, Mrs. O'Leary's.

The Challenge

Q: Where did the biggest fire of October 8, 1871, take place?

A: **In Peshtigo, Wisconsin.** On the same night as the Chicago fire, a forest fire burned through Peshtigo, a town of about 2,000 people, and the neighboring communities of Sugar Bush and Williamsville, taking 1,500 lives and over four million acres of forest and prairie. It was a terrible holocaust, with heat so intense that people taking refuge in the shallow river in Peshtigo were cinderized when they came up for air.

Chicago had a fairly extensive fire protection system in October 1871, but in the week before the fire, the department had fought twenty-four blazes, and on this Sunday night the equipment was being repaired and the personnel were resting. When the fire was first discovered in the barn belonging to Patrick and Catherine O'Leary at 137 De Koven Street, the city's alarm boxes were locked and most of the adjacent store-keepers, who were responsible for the keys, were asleep. Thus the fire got a real grip before the first hose was run out. A reporter, Michael Ahern, is said to have confessed to making up the cow-kicking story. As it is, the cow escaped the fire, for a neighbor got the O'Leary animals out in time. The human toll in Chicago, however, was a sad 250 lives.

The more jaded stat collectors are not impressed by the toll of the five-day Fire of London in 1666 (only four deaths) but are awed by the Tokyo-Yokohama Fire of 1923, where the count was just over 140,000! Yokohama was completely razed. No city, however, outdoes Istanbul, where a conflagration in 1729 (7,000 lives lost) was the first in a series of major fires that continued almost annually until the mid-twentieth century.

98

Q: For much of the eighteenth century, what was the most valuable export being shipped out of North America?

A: Of course, beaver pelts.

The Challenge

Q: What was the next most valuable export?

A. **Ginseng root.** Ultimately, fish and lumber became more valuable than ginseng, but cargo manifests and shipping reports of the time show that for a significant period (from about 1720 to 1760), ginseng exports were second only to furs in total value of product shipped.

In 1715, a Jesuit missionary in Quebec, Father Joseph-François Lafitau, realized that a medicinal root used by the Mohawk people (they called it *garantoquen*, meaning "man-like" or "shaped like a man") was the same stuff a colleague of his had written about in China. There it was called *jen-shen* (which means "man-like" or "shaped like a man") and was reputed to have significant medicinal powers. By 1720, the woods of modern-day New England, Ontario, and Quebec were being scoured for this forked root. Fur trappers dug it as a sideline, and for many of them – Daniel Boone was one – it often provided a better income than beaver pelts. Unfortunately, the root diggers were so thorough that by the time of the American Revolution the plant was almost extinct.

Especially in the Orient, ginseng is widely believed to have special qualities, although Western pharmacologists have found it difficult to identify precisely what these are. This is no more significant an Occidental failure than one undertaken by Western doctors in rural China in 1985. It was a U.N.-sponsored project to teach birth-control methods. Researchers discovered, after eighteen months of careful instruction in the use of condoms, that 97.4 percent of the Chinese farmers in the study were putting condoms on their index fingers, exactly as they had been shown during the demonstration meetings.

99

Q: In William Golding's novel *Lord of the Flies* (1954), what nearsighted character's thick glasses are used for starting a fire?

A: Right, Piggy's.

The Challenge

Q: Golding goofed here. Why?

A. **Glasses for correcting nearsightedness won't converge the sun's rays,** or start a fire. Both *Lord of the Flies* movies (England, 1963; U.S., 1990) repeat the error, but they were only following Golding's lead. No such excuse is handy for some other blunders that have appeared on the silver screen over the years. VCR "stop" and "replay" buttons will confirm these, for example:

- During what buffs regard as the definitive movie car chase, in *Bullitt* (1968), the Dodge Charger being pursued by Steve McQueen loses three hubcaps. Then it crashes and loses three more.
- The scoreboard clock in *Major League* (1989) shows 10:40 during a day game.
- Audrey Hepburn's legs are bare when she crawls through George Peppard's window in *Breakfast at Tiffany's* (1961) but then suddenly acquire black stockings.
- In *Nine to Five* (1980), a motorcycle cop stops Lily Tomlin because one rear light is out. When she drives away, both lights work.
- The number on Elvis Presley's prison togs in *Jailhouse Rock* (1957) grows from 6239 to 6240 at one point in the movie.
- *Indiana Jones and the Last Crusade* (1989) is set in 1938. In an airport lounge, two German passengers are shown reading newspapers from 1918.
- Near the end of *Forrest Gump* (1994), while at Jenny's grave, Tom Hanks says, "You died on a Saturday morning." But the date on her grave marker, March 22, 1982, is a Monday.
- Not a mistake in the classic sense, this one, but it deserves honorable mention in the category: D. W. Griffith made *The Battle of the Sexes* (1913) in four days. (A remake in 1928 took him four months.)

Q: One of the most unlikely kids' television stars ever, and an enduring one, was a rubbery little figure named Gumby, who appeared for years in a moralizing and – for adults – fantastically boring cartoon. What was the name of Gumby's horse?

A: Correct, Pokey.

The Challenge

Q: What was the name of Gumby's human friend?

A: **Bobby Nicholson.** Pokey, incidentally, was also the name of a Gene Autry sidekick (played by a human, Sterling Holloway) in several old western movies. Another occasional Autry companion was Gabby (George) Hayes. As a sidekick, Gabby really got around. He played companion to Roy Rogers, John Wayne, Hopalong Cassidy (for which Gabby's name was Windy Halliday), Wild Bill Elliott, and Randolph Scott. In every one of these roles, Gabby displayed an I.Q. level just a shade above that of his horse, but he was a symbol of unshakable loyalty, not to mention elective celibacy.

Pokey and Gumby owe far more to Charles Goodyear than they do to Gabby Hayes. On a February night in 1839, Goodyear was boiling rubber in the family kitchen. Although the Goodyears were extremely impoverished, this was not some nutritional extreme; Goodyear was trying to find a way to make rubber soft and pliant. By accident, he dropped a mixture of sulphur and melted rubber on the stovetop and didn't bother to wipe it up. The stove went out overnight, and in the morning Goodyear had a blob of "vulcanized" rubber. His gift to civilization never paid off for him, however. Goodyear died in poverty in 1860 with vulcanized rubber just a curiosity. About ten years later, Dr. Benjamin Franklin Goodrich — who knew about Goodyear's discovery — watched a friend's house burn to the ground one night because the fire department's leather hoses burst in the freezing cold. It didn't take long for Goodrich to persuade some well-heeled acquaintances to invest in his company. One of its first and most successful products was a hose made of vulcanized rubber.